CRYSTAL
GRIDWORK

CRYSTAL GRIDWORK

The Power of Crystals and Sacred Geometry to
Heal, Protect, and Inspire • KIERA FOGG

WEISER
BOOKS

To Our Readers

Weiser Books, an imprint of Red Wheel/Weiser, publishes books across the entire spectrum of occult, esoteric, speculative, and New Age subjects. Our mission is to publish quality books that will make a difference in people's lives without advocating any one particular path or field of study. We value the integrity, originality, and depth of knowledge of our authors.

Our readers are our most important resource, and we appreciate your input, suggestions, and ideas about what you would like to see published.

Visit our website at *www.redwheelweiser.com* to learn about our upcoming books and free downloads, and be sure to go to *www.redwheelweiser.com/newsletter* to sign up for newsletters and exclusive offers.

You can also contact us at *info@rwwbooks.com* or at Red Wheel/Weiser, LLC
65 Parker Street, Suite 7
Newburyport, MA 01950

A QUARTO BOOK
This edition first published in 2018 by Weiser Books, an imprint of
Red Wheel/Weiser, LCC
With offices at:
65 Parker Street, Suite 7
Newburyport, MA 01950
www.redwheelweiser.com

Copyright © 2018 Quarto Publishing plc
an imprint of The Quarto group

ISBN: 978-1-57863-642-6
Library of Congress Cataloging-in-Publication Data available upon request.

QUAR GRID

Conceived, edited, and designed by
Quarto Publishing
an imprint of The Quarto group
The Old Brewery
6 Blundell Street
London N7 9BH

Project editor Katie Crous
Designer Eoghan O' Brien
Photographer Phil Wilkins
Art director Caroline Guest
Creative director Moira Clinch
Publisher Samantha Warrington

Printed in China
10 9 8 7 6 5 4 3 2 1

Contents

MEET *Kiera*

I am a firm believer in the effect that healing crystals can have on our lives through the power of inspiration.

In October 2015, I launched an online shop that sends healing crystal collections for every occasion, similar to a flower shop sending bouquets. After only two months, my little crystal shop became a megahit in Hollywood and I began selling more crystal gift sets than I could keep up with. A year later, after having been featured in *Vogue*, *Forbes*, and *O, The Oprah Magazine*, and experiencing success beyond my wildest dreams, I found myself standing in my office, staring down at the healing crystal grid I had made for all of that! (I call it the Success Grid, and you will find exactly how I made it later in this book.)

The idea of finding the perfect geometrical shape to match the perfect combination of crystals can seem overwhelming to even the most advanced crystal collector. But crystal grids are not reserved for clairvoyants and professional energy workers. This healing modality, just like yoga and meditation, can be easily adapted by anyone. This book aims to empower you to become comfortable and confident in building your own crystal grids, from start to finish, so that you can be your own gridwork expert.

Crystals and grids

Aside from having my own meaningful experiences with healing crystals, I am constantly hearing stories of the powerful effects that crystals have had on people's lives. I've heard many remarkable tales of breakthroughs in careers, health, romances, and nearly every aspect of life.

A healing crystal grid combines the power of multiple crystals to build an energetic map that can guide us in the direction of our goals and create real and tangible changes in our lives. Furthermore, when we set our intentions through the use of a carefully created crystal grid, these changes can often happen quite fast.

A healing crystal grid builds an energetic map that can create real changes in our lives.

MEET KIERA

ABOUT THIS BOOK

I mmerse yourself in the world of healing crystals with this book. Start your journey by building a simple and inexpensive tool kit; discover the wonder and beauty of crystals as you progress; and end your journey by reaping the rewards of building successful and bespoke grids, tailored to your every need and desire.

CHAPTER 1:
Your Crystal Tool Kit

pages 10–29

At the core of your simple tool kit are, of course, your healing crystals. This chapter introduces you to the six key categories—Seeker, Attractor, Enhancer, Barrier, Guardian, and Dispeller Crystals—so that you can make an informed and relevant choice when it comes to selecting crystals for your own grids. Learn about their unique properties and how to unlock them.

CHAPTER 2:
Your Crystal Grid

pages 30–63

Learn how to build your own grids, where to place your crystals, and how to personalize your grids with meaningful added elements. With reference to sacred geometry, this section will also guide you through 12 principal grid formations, including Tripod of Life and Borromean Rings.

8

1. Further your knowledge with insights into each crystal category

2. Readily available examples of each crystal type

3. Up-close pictures show the beauty and variety of sample crystals

4. Deepen your understanding with background information and practical advice

5. Quick-glance overview of the grid's main uses

6. Clear line diagram of the grid formation, which you can photocopy or use as a base

Chapter 3:
30 Healing Crystal Grids to Change Your Life

pages 64–125

An indispensable source of 30 healing grids—complete with crystal details, positioning, and suggested enhancements—to cover a wide range of common desires, needs, and ailments. Use the page as a base on which to place your own crystals, as a tool for meditation and intention-setting, or as inspiration for your own version of the grid shown.

7. Summary of the grid's aims

8. Details of the grid put it in context and explain its uses and benefits

9. Gain insight into the main stones— Focus, Way, and Desire—and understand why each crystal has been selected

10. Suggested enhancements will help you get the most from your grid

11. The affirmations given will set your focus and lead you toward your goals

Place your crystals directly on top of those in the book (use smaller crystals if needed).

Photocopy or scan and print the grid, at a larger size if desired.

Or simply focus on the grid as a meditative aid and/or as a guide to setting your own intentions.

CHAPTER 1

YOUR CRYSTAL TOOL KIT

Becoming your own crystal grid expert does not have to be costly or complex. To get started, you will need only a handful of stones that suit your individual needs. In the following section, we will explore the real magic of crystals and how to select the most appropriate gems for your healing needs.

THE REAL MAGIC
OF CRYSTALS

Each holding their own unique meanings and energetic properties, healing crystals can act as amazing tools for improving health and wellness. This is exactly what they are: tools; and, like all tools, crystals are powerless without a willing and active user.

One of the most frequent questions I am asked, as a crystal shop owner, is, "Do crystals have magical powers?" Naturally, it can be hard for people to wrap their mind around a concept as far out as a rock having the power to change lives. My answer is always the same: I can't say for certain if the crystals themselves hold any magical powers beyond their symbolic representations, but I most certainly know that when paired with the human mind, I've seen them assist in accomplishing some pretty miraculous things.

CASE STUDY 1: *Sweet Dreams*

Kirsten's seven-year-old son, Tyson, had been having nightmares for several months. The situation had become so bad that his teachers began to notice angry and emotional outbursts at school due to his lack of sleep. Kirsten was gifted with a large, creamy Moonstone from our shop, which she passed on to Tyson. She told him it was his "dream rock." Tyson was encouraged to hold this stone to quiet his mind before bed. Kirsten suggested to him that if he woke up in the middle of the night, he should hold the rock and imagine it surrounding him with a protective shield of white light.

Not only did Tyson's nightmares stop, but he eventually revealed that he was feeling anxious from being picked on at school. Kirsten was able to address the issue with his teachers, and Tyson is now thriving at school and at home.

CASE STUDY 2: *A Message from the Angels*

Joni's father had recently passed and she was feeling increasingly distraught. Raised by her father, a single dad, she felt completely alone without him. Soon after his passing, she was sent a crystal gift set from a friend containing a piece of Angelite, a stone known for its connection to the spirit world. The gift-message read, "Forever and always his little Button," a nickname he had given her as a child. Joni tucked the Angelite crystal in her purse.

One month later she called her friend, ecstatic. Soon after receiving her gift, she started seeing buttons everywhere. She would find them on the sidewalk when she was out for a jog, in the grass near her father's graveside, and even in her purse, right next to her special stone. She now keeps her collection of buttons with her very special piece of Angelite.

13

YOU ARE THE POWER

Setting your intentions is by far the most critical step in building your crystal grid. It is only by way of setting compelling, spiritually aligned intentions that our grids can hold any real power at all. Furthermore, research has shown that change is most likely to occur when we focus on changing one habit at a time. This is why I suggest setting one clearly defined intention for each crystal grid that you build.

Exercise: Focusing Attention

This exercise is designed to help you identify which areas of life need your attention the most. On a scale of 1 to 10 (1 being "I strongly disagree" and 10 being "I strongly agree"), write the number that is true for you next to each of the following statements:

◊ I feel secure

◊ I feel physically healthy

◊ I feel focused

◊ I feel loved

◊ I feel confident

◊ I feel at peace

◊ I feel spiritually connected

◊ I feel successful

◊ I feel blessed

◊ I feel lucky

◊ I feel financially free

◊ I feel creative

◊ I feel strong

1
TUNE IN

Set aside some time to sit quietly by yourself. Close your eyes, and simply allow yourself to feel all the physical and emotional sensations that arise.

2
TAKE NOTE

What do you notice? Is your throat tight? Do you have butterflies in your stomach? Are you having trouble focusing? Make a list of everything you notice and then ask yourself, "What do I need the most right now?"

3
FOCUS

Narrow your list down to one key area of focus. If you are not sure which observation is the most important, ask yourself, "What hurts the most?"

4
WRITE YOUR "I AM" STATEMENT

Your "I am" statement is your new intention, stated as if it has already happened. For example: "I express myself with complete confidence."

SELECTING THE RIGHT CRYSTALS

If you've ever visited a crystal shop, you might have had a funny feeling that even though you had arrived with the intention of choosing your crystals, the sparkling array of gems were actually in the process of choosing you.

I have watched hundreds of people select crystals from my shop, and it truly amazes me to witness the powerful energetic pull that crystals can have on people. It seems that our customers tend to select intuitively the exact right gems for their current healing needs. Similarly, you might find yourself instinctively drawn to a specific type of crystal when building your grid, and, when this is the case, I always suggest that you go with your gut instinct. Your intuition is always the best indicator of what you truly need.

However, there are some more concrete insights that we can use to guide us in selecting the best crystals for our grids. With the help of modern scientific instruments, we are able to see the exact molecular makeup of the various types of healing crystals. These molecular structures indicate why certain types of crystals seem to provoke certain feelings and reactions.

There are six main categories that crystals fall into, and it is through the understanding of these six different types of crystal energy lattices that we can identify the circumstances in which they should be used.

1	2	3	4	5	6
Seeker Crystals (pages 18–19)	Attractor Crystals (pages 20–21)	Enhancer Crystals (pages 22–23)	Guardian Crystals (pages 24–25)	Barrier Crystals (pages 26–27)	Dispeller Crystals (pages 28–29)

    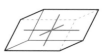 

BEST CLEANSING METHOD

Healing crystals have the tendency to pick up and retain energy, so it is important to cleanse them frequently. There are many different ways to cleanse your crystals, but the "white light" method of cleansing is my favorite, because it doesn't require anything special other than your own direct focus.

1. Hold your crystals in the palms of your hands and close your eyes.

2. Take a few deep breaths and imagine that a bright white light is radiating from the palms of your hands and enveloping your crystals.

3. When you have this image in your mind's eye, simply say the following prayer:

"These crystals are cleansed and released of all lower energies. They are recharged with their natural properties, and are ready to be used in divine healing now."

SEEKER *Crystals*

Manifesting goals and desires

O ne of the most unifying human characteristics is the fact that we are always seeking something new. Whether it is a new career, new love, better health, increased self-confidence, or any number of other desires we have for improvement, there is one thing for certain: we all have a need to expand and improve. In fact, consider for a moment the very reason you picked up this book. Chances are it was because you were hoping to create a new result of some kind. Therefore, when it comes to building crystal grids, Seeker Crystals are often the most useful, because these are the crystals that help us to find and attract the new.

Seeker Crystals have an internal molecular structure that is hexagonal in shape. When broken down even further, the hexagon shape consists of triangular or pointed patterns resembling arrows. Quite naturally, this type of crystal is used to provide direction, or "point the way." Like an arrow aimed at its target, the Seeker leads us in the direction in which we wish to go.

CHOOSE the Seeker Crystal for your grid any time you would like to manifest a new result of some kind—from finding love, through forming new habits, to manifesting goals—as the energy of these crystals inspires us to find new horizons, break through barriers, and create favorable circumstances for what we desire.

Amethyst (4)	*Citrine (3)*	*Rose Quartz (1)*
Aquamarine	*Clear Quartz (2)*	*Ruby*
Aventurine (7)	*Emerald*	*Sapphire*
Beryl	*Hematite*	*Sardonyx*
Blue Lace Agate (5)	*Jasper*	*Tiger's Eye (6)*
Calcite	*Mookaite*	*Tourmaline*
Carnelian	*Morganite*	
Chalcedony	*Onyx*	
Cinnabar	*Rhodochrosite*	

ATTRACTOR *Crystals*

Becoming a magnet for our desires · Attracting miracles of all kinds

Attractor Crystals are very powerful additions to a crystal grid. Similar to the Seeker, which offers us the energy to go out and find what we want, the Attractor offers a magnetic energy that helps us to draw in our desires.

Formed in the Tetragonal crystal system, these gems contain an internal structure that is built on the rectangle, and they tend to be especially shiny in appearance. Because of their ability to catch the eye, they are believed to inspire this same alluring appeal in us.

Because the Attractor acts like a magnet, drawing in all that surrounds it, it should only be used when paired with other crystals like the Seeker: if there is nothing around it to attract, its energy will remain dormant, waiting for something to draw in. Pair it with the Seeker to inspire you to find what you want, and then become a complete magnet for attaining it.

USE the Attractor Crystal on your grid for help with becoming a magnet for your desires. This is the type of energy that helps us to establish influence, gain friends, attract fame, and attain fortune of all kinds.

Apophyllite (1)
Carletonite
Cassiterite
Chalcopyrite (2)
Leucite
Marialite

Phosgenite
Powellite
Pyrolusite
Rutile Smoky Quartz (3)

Scapolite
Scheelite
Stolzite
Vesuvianite (4)
Zircon (5)

ATTRACTOR CRYSTALS

ENHANCER *Crystals*

Improving circumstances · Magnifying success · Self-improvement

I f the crystal world had a self-help aisle, we would find rows and rows of beautiful Enhancer Crystals. Much like a great self-help book, these crystals offer an energy that urges us to improve on our current strengths, assets, and positive circumstances, helping us to harvest more of the good that already exists in our lives.

Enhancers are those crystals that fall into the category of the Isometric crystal system. These crystals hold an internal energy lattice that consists of perfectly symmetrical cubes. Because of this, Enhancers are often referred to as the "building block" crystals.

Allow the energy of the Enhancer Crystal to inspire you to live life at your very best.

22

CHOOSE the Enhancer Crystal for your grid when you wish to build upon your current circumstances—from improving your mental or physical health, through attaining more success in your career, to enhancing your relationships.

Andradite	Garnet	Sperrylite
Bornite	Halite	Spessartine
Chlorargyrite	Lapis Lazuli (3)	Spinel
Chromite	Lazurite	Sulfur
Cuprite	Magnetite	Sylvite
Diamond	Peacock Ore (5)	Tsavorite
Dravite	Pyrite (1)	Uvarovite
Fluorite (4)	Pyrope	
Galena	Sodalite (2)	

ENHANCER CRYSTALS

GUARDIAN *Crystals*

Maintaining current circumstances · Protecting what we have

In the physical world, when we have something we want to protect, we take special measures. We build fences, install windows, and activate alarm systems. We know that it is important to keep our valuable possessions out of harm's way. Similarly, Guardian Crystals bring a protective energy to your grid.

Guardian Crystals are those that form in the Monoclinic crystal system. Their internal crystalline structures are made up of parallel lines, offering an energetic shield of protection between ourselves and undesirable circumstances.

Very powerful when paired with Enhancers, Guardian Crystals are intended to magnify what we already have. When combined on a grid, Guardians and Enhancers will work together to protect and improve our current circumstances.

24

IF you have a particular area of life you wish to keep safe, try lining the outer edges of your grid with a row of Guardians. These gems are great for protecting our homes, loved ones, and our physical security.

Alabaster (7)	*Gypsum*	*Preseli Bluestone*
Azurite	*Howlite (6)*	*Realgar*
Charoite (4)	*Jade*	*Rosasite*
Chrysocolla (5)	*Jadeite*	*Selenite (1)*
Creedite	*Kunzite*	*Serpentine*
Datolite	*Lazulite*	*Spirit Quartz*
Desert Rose (8)	*Lepidolite (2)*	*Stilbite*
Epidote	*Malachite (3)*	
Fuchsite	*Muscovite*	

BARRIER *Crystals*

Preventing misfortune · Protection from negativity

Similar to the Guardian Crystal, Barrier Crystals are also used on a grid for the purpose of protection. However, Barriers are a little different in that they are intended to shield us from what we do not have nor do not want, while the Guardians are focused on protecting and maintaining what we already have.

Containing a Triclinic crystal structure, the energy lattice of a Barrier does not contain any right angles. Instead, Barriers are formed across all directions of their internal shapes, making them extremely powerful stones for protection.

Allow Barrier Crystals to act as the sole protectors on your grid, or pair them with Guardians and these gems will work together to maintain what you have and shield you from unnecessary mishaps.

26

USE the Barrier Crystal to protect against misfortunes of all kinds, including illness, accidents, financial loss, heartbreak, and the unknown.

Amazonite (4)	*Larimar (3)*	*Turquoise*
Andesine	*Microcline*	*Ulexite*
Bustamite	*Moonstone (2)*	*Wulfenite*
Bytownite	*Pectolite*	
Epistilbite	*Pyroxmangite*	
Inesite	*Rhodonite*	
Kyanite (5)	*Serandite*	
Labradorite (1)	*Sunstone*	

BARRIER CRYSTALS

DISPELLER *Crystals*

Eliminating unwanted circumstances · Restoring harmony

If the Dispeller Crystal had a mantra, it would be "Out with the old, in with the new." And, as we know, a healthy part of any growth cycle is the peaceful release of that which is no longer serving us. Dispellers can be very effective in inspiring us to let go of old and unwanted patterns, experiences, and feelings.

Forming under the Orthorhombic system, Dispellers have an internal molecular structure that appears in the shape of diamonds. These diamonds consist of multiple outward-facing points that are said to be helpful in directing negative energy away from its source—us!

Allow the energy of the Dispeller to help restore a sense of harmony and balance in your life.

28

USE the Dispeller Crystal on your grid any time you wish to cleanse, detoxify, or release an old pattern in your life. Dispellers can inspire us to rid ourselves of worry, stress, toxic relationships, financial difficulty, and many other troublesome areas of life.

Adamite	Chrysoberyl	Prehnite
Andalusite	Danburite	Stibnite
Anglesite	Dumortierite	Tanzanite
Anhydrite	Goethite	Topaz
Aragonite (3)	Hemimorphite	Variscite
Barite	Iolite (4)	Zoisite (2)
Bronzite (1)	Natrolite	
Brookite	Olmiite	
Celestite (5)	Peridot	

DISPELLER CRYSTALS

Chapter 2

YOUR CRYSTAL GRID

Now that you have created the crystal tool kit that's right for you, let's take a closer look at putting it all together. In this chapter, we delve into the fascinating world of sacred geometry and explore what it takes to start building a crystal grid that best represents your own unique dreams and desires.

THE POWER OF GEOMETRY

Take a close look at any flower, leaf, horned animal, beehive, feather, or pinecone and you will notice something truly spectacular. In these products of nature, you will see patterns that are perfectly symmetrical, repeating and aligning in complete, divine harmony.

Often referred to as "sacred geometry," our Universe is made up of shapes that can be found repeated in various natural formations. When broken down to their finest components, a geometrical shape is merely a pattern repeated in harmonious proportions. It is with the use of these sacred shapes that mankind has been able to build impressive historical structures. The Ancient Greeks and Egyptians used these patterns to build tombs and temples that stand to this day—and we can use the very same patterns, too.

Crystal gridwork builds on sacred patterns to bring the natural divine order of the Universe to our crystal grids. Each holding unique meanings, sacred shapes such as the Spiral, Seed of Life, Star of David, Vesica Piscis, and so on, have the power to inspire your grid in a different way. When chosen and applied correctly, these shapes work with the energy lattices of our crystals, to inspire positive change in our lives.

There are 12 main grid formations that we look at in this book:

1. Seed of Life
(pages 40–41)

2. Flower of Life
(pages 42–43)

3. Vesica Piscis
(pages 44–45)

4. Circle
(pages 46–47)

5. Spiral
(pages 48–49)

6. Triangle
(pages 50–51)

7. Square
(pages 52–53)

8. Cross
(pages 54–55)

9. Star of David
(pages 56–57)

10. Ashoka Chakra
(pages 58–59)

11. Borromean Rings
(pages 60–61)

12. Tripod of Life
(pages 62–63)

33

HOW TO BUILD
A CRYSTAL GRID

Here is an easy, step-by-step guide to building your own crystal grid.

1
SET YOUR INTENTIONS

Decide which area of life you want to make changes to over the next 40 days, then write your one- or two-sentence "I am" statement (see page 14) on a small piece of paper.

2
SELECT YOUR SHAPE

Select a shape that best represents the core desires of your "I am" statement. For example, if your statement is "I am attracting and saving large sums of money," you might choose the Seed of Life, as it is known to help manifest financial abundance. See pages 40–63 for suggested grid shapes.

3
SELECT YOUR STONES

Using both the guidance of your own intuition and the insights in this book, select the best healing crystals to represent the Focus Stone, Way Stones, and the Desire Stones for your grid. See pages 10–29 for more information on crystals.

MAKE IT PERSONAL

Decorate your grid with anything that inspires you. This might include special objects like jewelry, feathers, shells, or plants. See pages 38–39 for more ideas.

CHOOSE PLACEMENT AND LOCATION

Choose a location that best suits the intention of your grid. For instance, a Romance Grid (pages 90–91) would go well in a bedroom, while a Success Grid (pages 78–79) could be best built in an office.

PREPARE YOUR CRYSTALS

Cleanse and recharge your crystals. See page 17 for an easy and effective cleansing method.

PLACE AND ACTIVATE YOUR GRID

Place the piece of paper containing your "I am" statement underneath your Focus Stone. Build the rest of your grid in the shape you chose in step 2. Finally, activate your grid by using a Clear Quartz wand or point to trace an imaginary line connecting all of the crystals together.

Your grid should remain untouched for at least 40 days.

EMBELLISH YOUR GRID: *If you wish, you can embellish your grid with natural seasonal decorations and other objects that resonate with you.*

PLACING YOUR CRYSTALS

A t first glance, the crystal placement on a grid might seem merely like great aesthetics, but there is much more to it than meets the eye.

There are three different crystal positions to fill on a grid. These are referred to as the Focus Stone, Way Stone, and Desire Stone, and how you choose to fill these three positions will depend on how you wish to channel and direct the energy of your grid.

Focus Stone

Found most often at the center of your grid, the Focus Stone channels and gathers the creative power of the Universe to your grid, before sending it along an energetic pathway toward the Way and Desire Stones. While any type of crystal will work, typically your Focus Stone will be a larger stone, such as a cluster, point, or carved shape. If you are unsure which crystal to use, a Clear Quartz point or cluster is always a safe bet as a Focus Stone.

Way Stone

Most often consisting of tumbled stones or points that are arranged in the area immediately surrounding the Focus Stone, the Way Stones create a pathway toward your end result. When choosing your Way Stone, ask yourself, "How am I going to get there?" Will it be by way of courage? Clear communication? Self-love? Knowing the answers will help you to choose the most useful Way Stones.

Desire Stone

Typically consisting of tumbled stones or points arranged around the outer edges of your grid, the Desire Stone is the one most closely associated with your goal. When choosing your Desire Stone, simply ask yourself, "What do I desire?" Is it financial wealth? Self-confidence? Romance? The answer will help you to decide on the perfect fit for your Desire Stone.

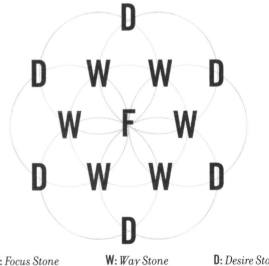

F: *Focus Stone*   **W:** *Way Stone*   **D:** *Desire Stone*

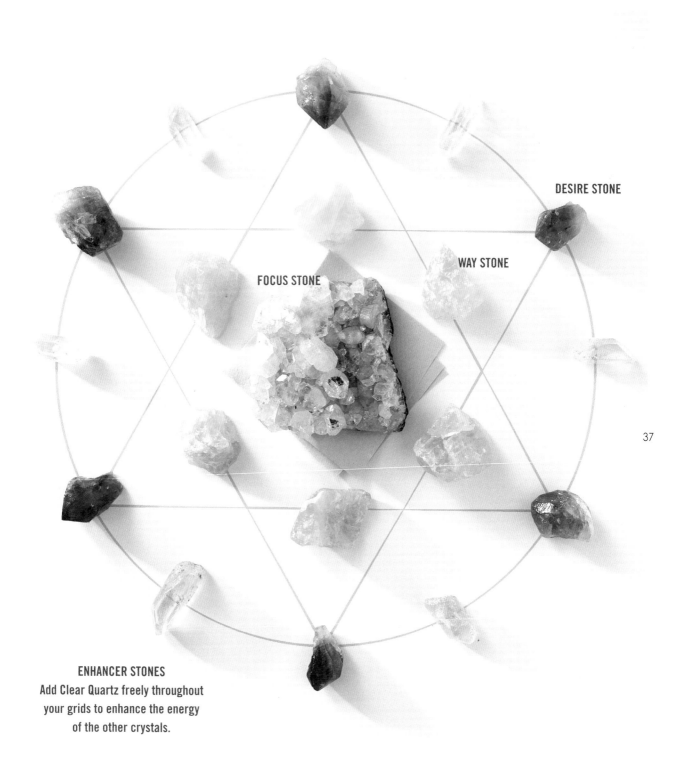

DESIRE STONE

WAY STONE

FOCUS STONE

37

ENHANCER STONES
Add Clear Quartz freely throughout
your grids to enhance the energy
of the other crystals.

MAKE IT PERSONAL

Throughout Chapter 3 you will see that many of the crystal grids have been decorated with special objects that bring additional meaning. While you may choose to add these items to your own grid, they are certainly not required. Feel free to embellish your grid with objects that inspire you, or allow the crystals to stand alone in their beauty. On these two pages are some examples of items you might choose to include.

SEASHELLS carry the energy of the ocean, and are a wonderful symbol for peace and harmony.

FEATHERS can be added to represent angelic guidance, wisdom, and insight.

PHOTOGRAPHS are wonderful additions when building relationship-focused grids.

JEWELRY can be added to include a personalized element to your grid.

38

FLOWERS AND FOLIAGE bring the element of growth and rejuvenation to your grid. Choose vibrant colors to invoke power, strength, and energy; lighter colors to invoke serenity. Leave fresh flowers and any other fresh elements to dry naturally for the duration of the grid (40 days)—they should not be replaced.

39

SEED OF LIFE

One of the most common and useful shapes associated with crystal grids is the "Seed of Life," which is best used for manifesting actionable desires.

Consisting of seven intertwining circles that come together to form a flower-like effect, this shape is sometimes associated with the six days of Creation and is likened to the appearance of cells dividing. Along with its highly creative energy, the repetition of spheres signifies balance, harmony, and protection. Use the Seed of Life to form your grid any time you wish to see a task through to completion or accomplish a goal of any kind. An additional circle can be drawn around the rim and lined with Guardian or Dispeller Crystals (see pages 24 and 28) for an extra barrier of protection when desired.

USE THIS SHAPE TO:

· Manifest dreams and goals

· See any task or project through to completion

· Maintain energy and stamina

· Build new habits and strengthen willpower

· Enhance creativity

· Attract good luck and abundance

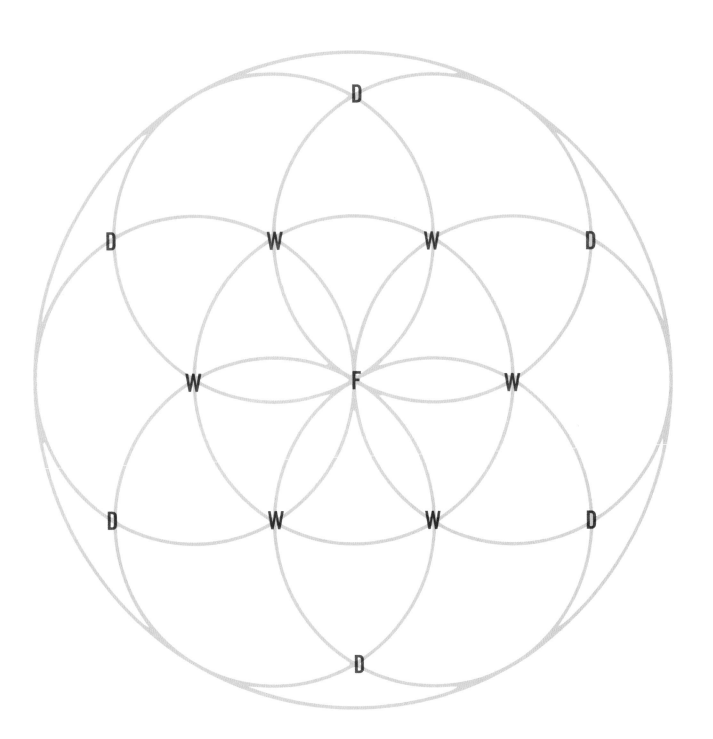

FLOWER OF LIFE

The Flower of Life is a commonly used expanded version of the Seed of Life. In fact, many other sacred symbols, such as the Tripod of Life, the Vesica Piscis, and Metatron's Cube, can also be found hidden away within this intricate shape.

Consisting of 19 intertwining circles, we can see this shape manifested repeatedly in nature—in snowflakes, crystals, the division of cells, and flowers. It is for this reason that the Flower of Life is believed to contain within it the blueprint of the Universe.

The Flower of Life is considered a very powerful "good for anything" shape, so it is a safe bet any time you are unsure of which shape to choose for your grid. Much like the Seed of Life, the Flower of Life is known to hold the energy of harmony, balance, creation, manifestation, and renewal. Use this shape when you wish to manifest a new result of some kind. It is also especially good for introspection, as it helps to promote knowledge, wisdom, and self-esteem.

USE THIS SHAPE TO:

- Promote knowledge and inner awareness

- Increase confidence and self-esteem

- Manifest goals and desires

- Restore harmony and balance

- Enhance creativity

- Attract wealth and abundance

42

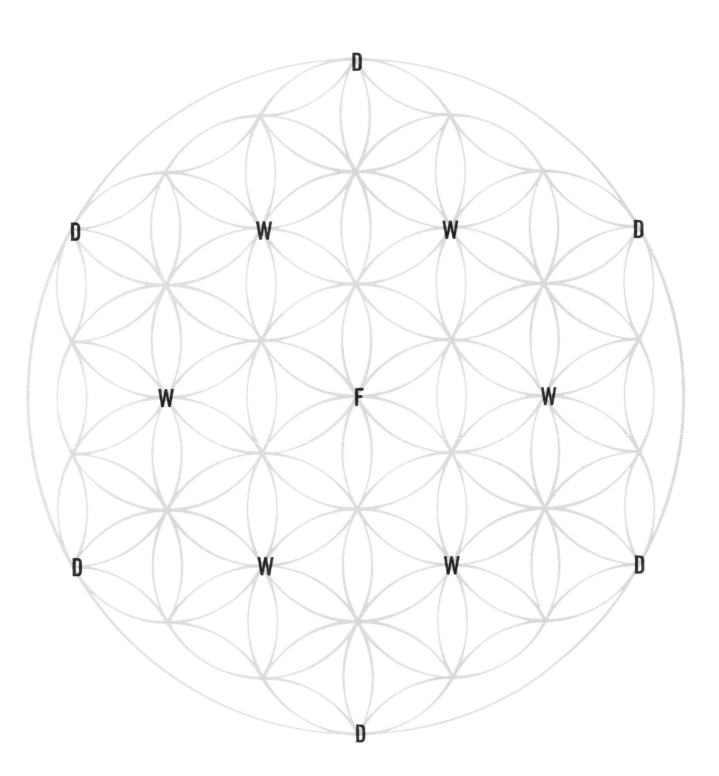

VESICA PISCIS

Formed out of two circles intertwining, the Vesica Piscis is an ancient symbol for balance, rebirth, and harmony.

At the center of the two connecting circles is a shape that you might recognize as the commonly used symbol found in Christianity to represent the fish, Christ, and the bridging of the spiritual and physical worlds. Because of this, it is a powerful symbol for enhancing unity and connection.

Use the Vesica Piscis to form your grid any time you wish to build a connection or bridge a gap, as the uniting circles will help you to find balance and connection in the middle ground of any situation.

44

USE THIS SHAPE TO:

· Improve relationships

· Inspire harmony and balance

· Promote understanding

· Connect with others and your higher self

· Promote rebirth and transformation

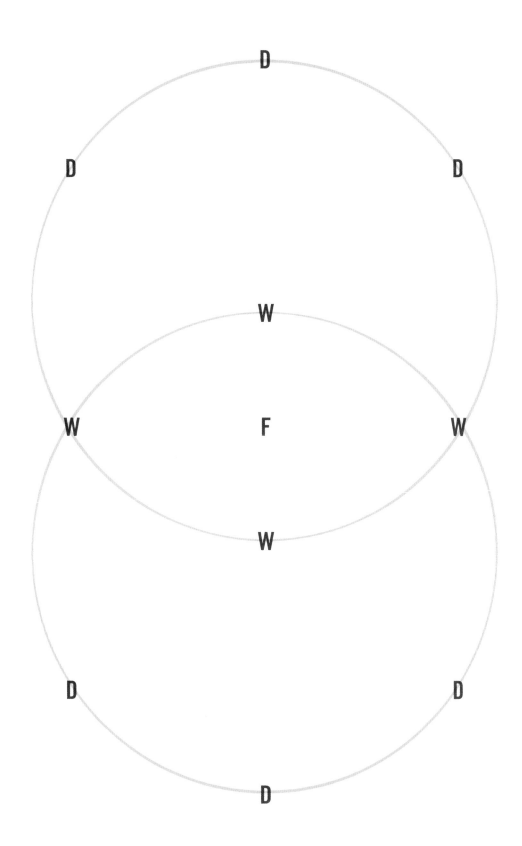

CIRCLE

You might not think of this shape as being all that special or powerful, but don't be fooled—there is great power to be found in its simplicity.

If you are married, look down at your ring finger. There is a reason we use this sacred shape as a universal symbol for our most important life commitments.

Holding the energy for unity, completion, and oneness, the Circle represents the infinite support of the Universe. Having no beginning and no end, this simple shape can inspire constancy, stability, and wellbeing. When used to build our grids it brings us connection, divine flow, renewal, support, and protection.

USE THIS SHAPE TO:

· Strengthen friendships and commitments

· Promote security and protection

· Inspire a sense of inner peace and connection with the Universe

· Invite feelings of renewal, clarity, and wellbeing

46

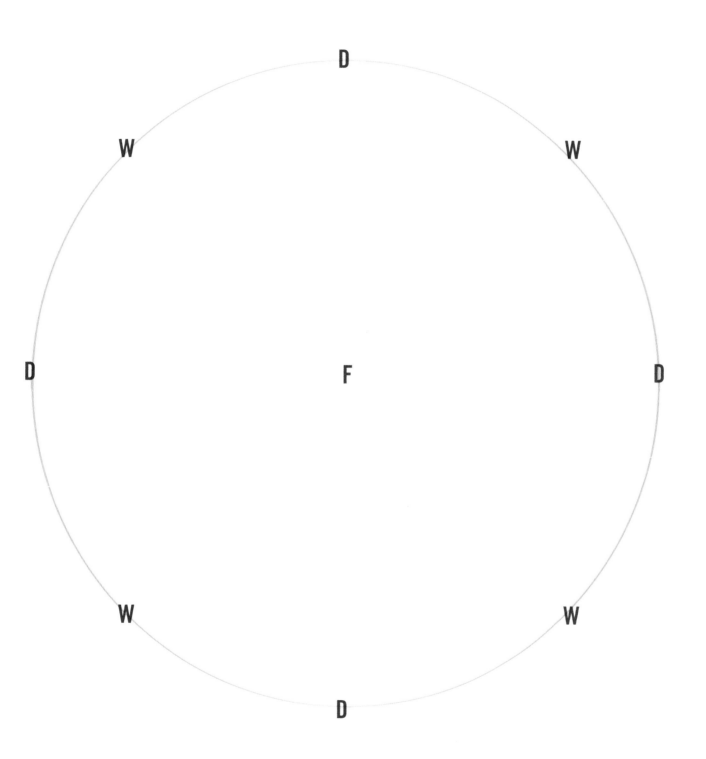

SPIRAL

Starting at a single point and expanding outward to infinity, the spiral can be seen as a representation of our ever-expanding Universe.

Acting as a primary structure for various growth patterns found in nature, the Spiral can be seen in the coiled snake, horned animals, colonies of fish, fossils, storm patterns, galaxies, seashells, and even in our own strands of DNA.

Use the Spiral to benefit from the universal law of Expansion, allowing this powerful shape to support personal growth and development of any kind. Because of its special ties to the physical world, it can also be useful for improving our health and reestablishing a sense of balance and wellbeing.

48

USE THIS SHAPE TO:

- Improve health

- Enhance stamina and focus

- Provide a sense of grounding

- Expand knowledge and heighten consciousness

- Support personal growth of any kind

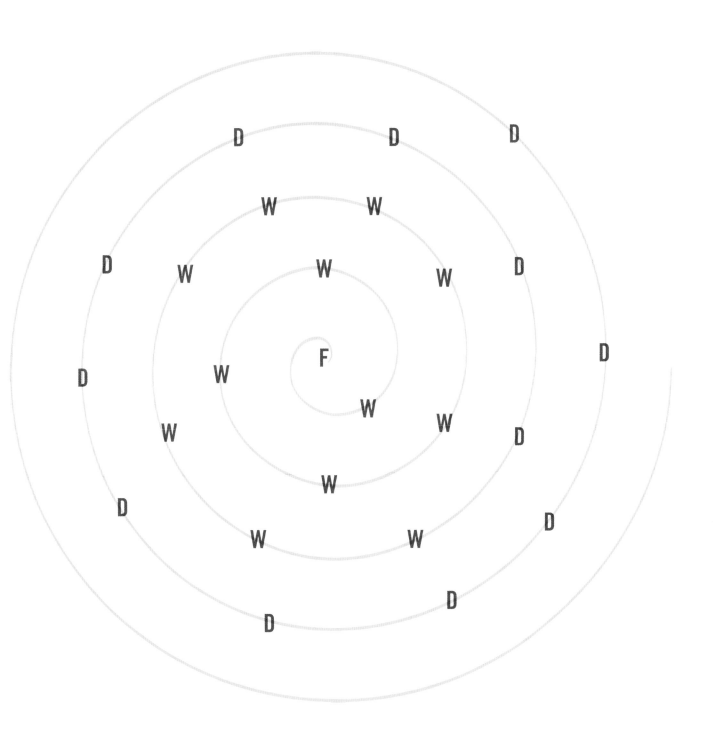

TRIANGLE

Consisting of three lines and three points, the Triangle is often associated with the union of the mind, body, and spirit.

The Triangle can provide our grids with the power of elevation, as the upward-facing point can be helpful in raising our perceptions and connecting us to higher levels of consciousness. It is an especially useful shape for gaining spiritual wisdom and enhancing divine communication.

Use the Triangle to build your grid when you wish to heighten your awareness, enhance intuition, and improve creativity. It is also known to be helpful in raising our energetic frequencies, so build your grid in a triangular shape any time you feel off kilter mentally, spiritually, or physically.

USE THIS SHAPE TO:

· Connect with higher wisdom

· Increase psychic abilities

· Enhance divine communication

· Inspire peace and clarity

· Improve creativity

· Manifest new desires

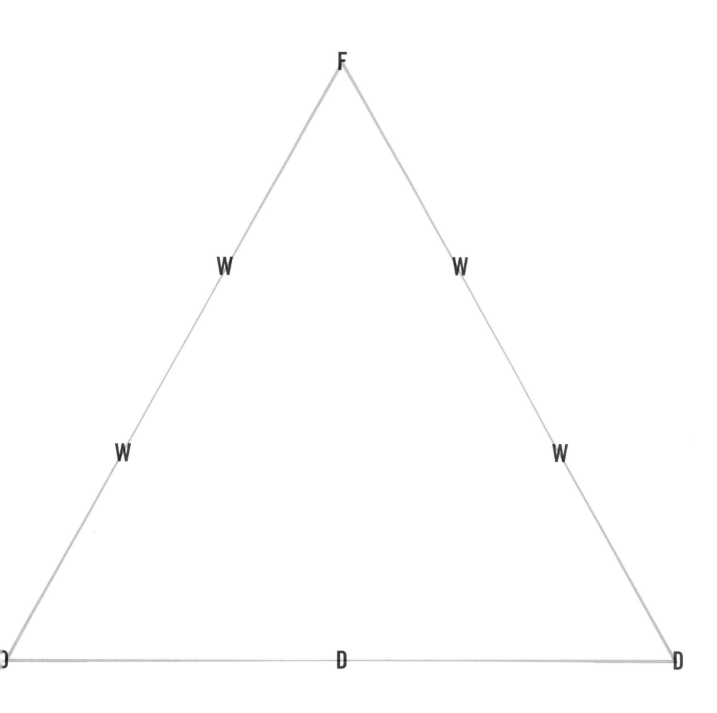

SQUARE

Offering intense strength, the Square is one of the most powerful shapes in sacred geometry. With four sides of equal parts, the Square is symbolic of the world's physical boundaries.

There is a reason we build our houses in the shape of squares: this shape helps us to know our limits, set boundaries, provide a sense of security, and build solid foundations. At the same time, it offers a sense of confidence in knowing that we are safe in our connection to the earth. In nature, squares can be found in the molecular makeup of some of the most common crystals, from iron pyrite and galena, to good old-fashioned table salt. Squares are also commonly associated with the four seasons (Summer, Winter, Spring, Fall), the four directions (North, South, East, West), and the four elements of Earth (Earth, Water, Air, Fire).

Use the Square to form your grid when you feel yourself needing a boost of strength, self-confidence, or stability. The Square is a very powerful grid to use for protection, and is especially helpful in enabling us to set reasonable boundaries.

USE THIS SHAPE TO:

- Set and maintain personal boundaries
- Inspire a sense of safety and protection
- Build on goals and dreams
- Improve self-confidence
- Enhance feelings of stability and security

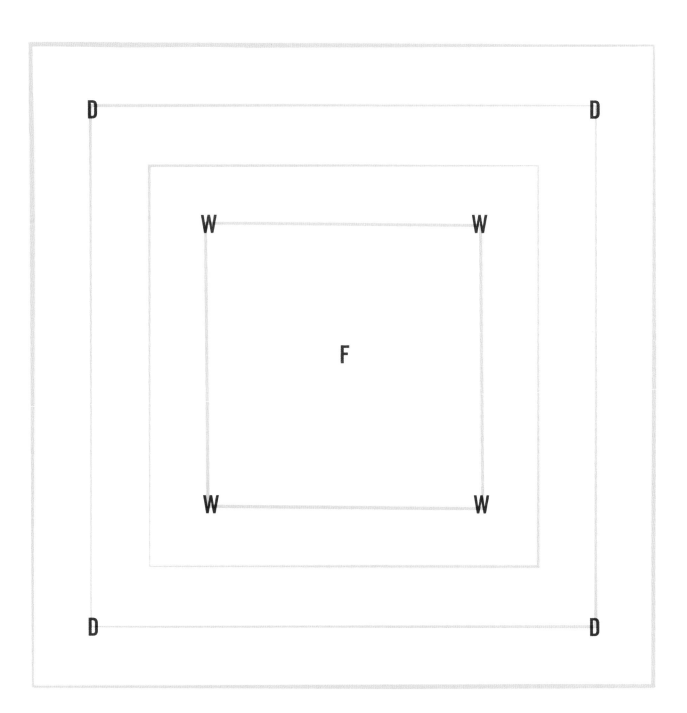

CROSS

Used as a protective symbol across many different cultures and religions for thousands of years, the Cross is associated with the intersecting of the physical and spiritual worlds.

The Cross is an especially useful shape for when we are seeking wisdom from the spirit world. It can also be a powerful shape for helping us to atone for our errors, as its converging paths can inspire us to see clearly from opposing perspectives.

Use the Cross to form your grid when you wish to deepen your faith, or make things right, as it is known to be helpful in both strengthening our belief systems and inspiring us to make necessary adjustments in our lives. Furthermore, being an ancient symbol for protection, this is also a very useful shape to guard against negative energy.

USE THIS SHAPE TO:

- Seek or offer forgiveness
- Atone, or make things right
- Connect to the spiritual world
- Build faith and strengthen belief systems
- Seek protection and dispel negative energy

54

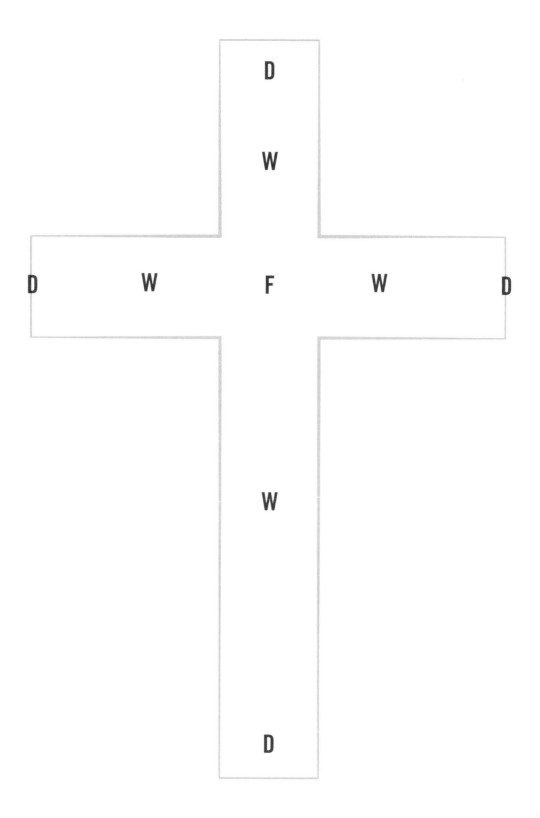

STAR OF DAVID

Most widely known as a Judaic symbol, the Star of David consists of two triangles converging from opposite directions to create a six-point star.

The merging of the two triangles can act as a powerful call for harmony and union within us, as it represents the uniting of the spiritual and physical worlds. We see the Star of David, which is also known as the Hexagon, repeated in nature in crystals, honeycombs, and snowflakes.

The Star of David is a versatile shape suitable for many different purposes, and can be applied wherever more harmony is needed. Use the Star of David to build your grid any time you wish to bring peace and balance to a situation. If you are feeling stressed or anxious, this is a particularly useful shape. It can also be helpful in deepening levels of connection and cooperation in relationships.

56

USE THIS SHAPE TO:

- Restore balance and harmony

- Inspire spiritual connection

- Improve cooperation in relationships

- Alleviate stress and anxiety

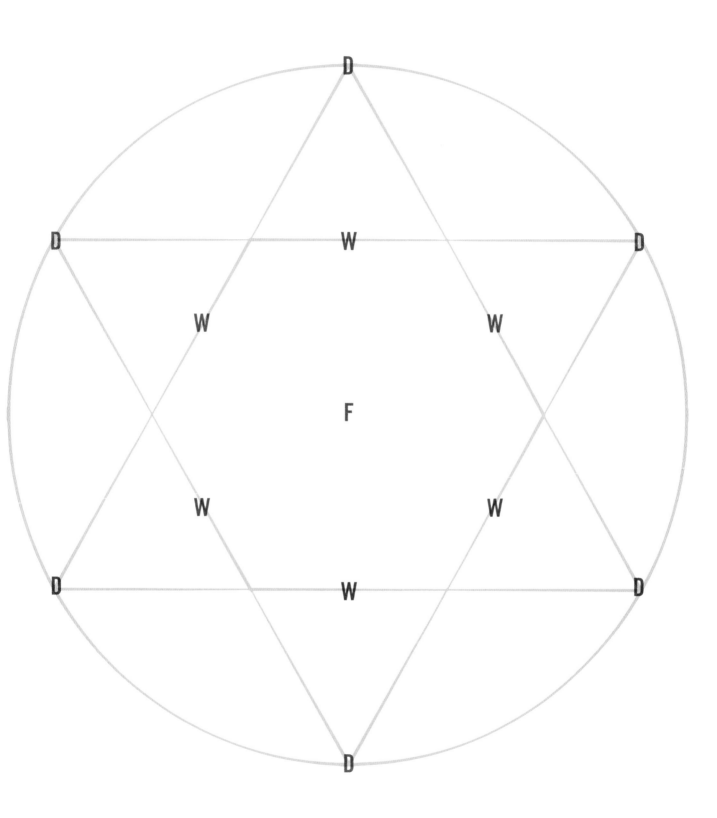

ASHOKA CHAKRA

The beautiful Ashoka Chakra is a variation of the Buddhist symbol for the *dharmachakra*, also known as the Wheel of Dharma.

Most visible on India's national flag, the 24 spokes on the wheel-like shape of the Ashoka Chakra are known to represent 24 sacred virtues and a 24-hour cycle of time.

Use the Ashoka Chakra to shape your grid when you wish to improve your character by strengthening your commitment to your highest moral virtues. This very powerful shape creates an energetic channel for helping us to become the people we wish to be. Use it to deepen faith, boost strength, promote courage, inspire resilience, build patience, or embody any other virtue you can think of.

USE THIS SHAPE TO:

- Develop moral virtues of all kinds

- Align your will with that of your creator

- Promote patience by embracing the cycle of time

- Release stress and anxiety

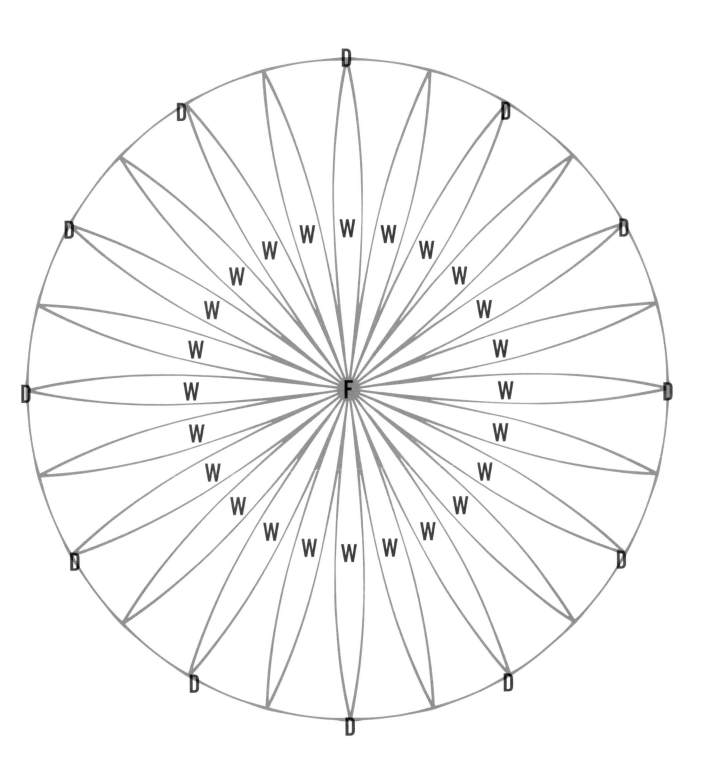

BORROMEAN RINGS

An ancient symbol for unity, the Borromean Rings consists of three interlocking circles that if broken at any given part would cause the entire shape to collapse and fall away.

Sometimes referred to as the Trinity Rings, this shape is known to symbolize our link to the Holy Spirit and our fellow neighbor.

Due to its link to both divine and human connection, the Borromean Rings is a very versatile shape. Use it to build your grid when you wish to achieve a miracle, as the basis for all miracles begins with the ability to see no separation between others and ourselves. This is also a very powerful shape to use when working in a group to achieve a common goal. Use the Borromean Rings to help alleviate or prevent tension, and inspire cooperation and harmony.

60

USE THIS SHAPE TO:

· Offer support in matters related to friendships, work, or family

· Inspire teamwork and cooperation

· Alleviate tension

· Deepen all forms of connection

· Invoke miracles of all kinds

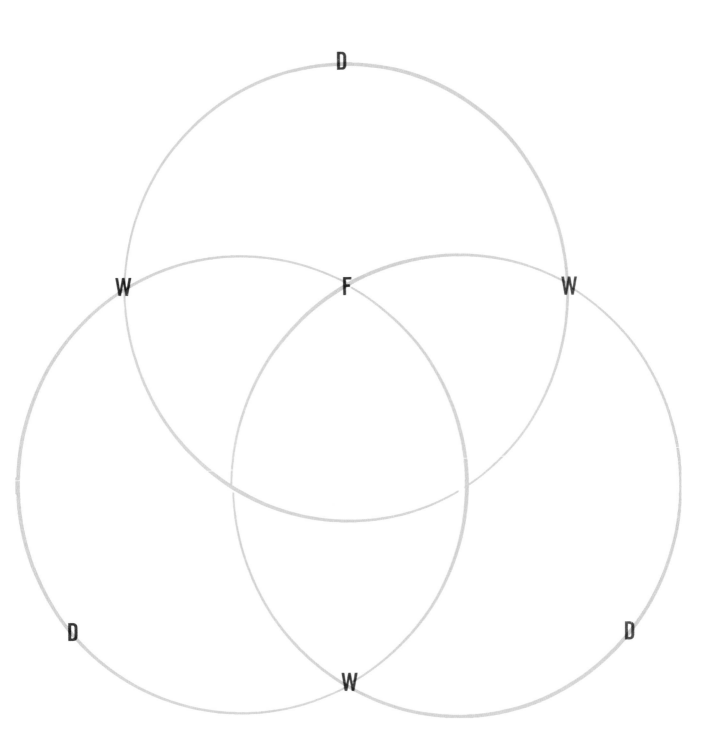

TRIPOD OF LIFE

Looking very much like a curved triangle, the Tripod of Life is often referred to as the "pregnant triangle."

The Tripod of Life is found within various geometrical shapes including the Seed of Life, the Flower of Life, and directly at the center of the Borromean Rings. Because of this, it is said to offer much of the same creative energies, but in a more concentrated and focused way. The rings from which it is made appear to have fallen away, leaving only the shape's core. The Tripod of Life offers a similar effect to our grids, allowing us to cut away all of that which no longer serves us.

Use the Tripod of Life to build your grid when you wish to inspire a laser-like focus on any area of life. It can also be used to supercharge our creative energies, as it enables us to see past the clutter of the mind and focus only on the goal. Furthermore, it is known to be helpful in matters related to family, romantic relationships, and fertility.

USE THIS SHAPE TO:

- Start a family
- Bring a new project or venture to life
- Boost creativity
- Build an intense romantic connection
- Begin a new journey of any kind

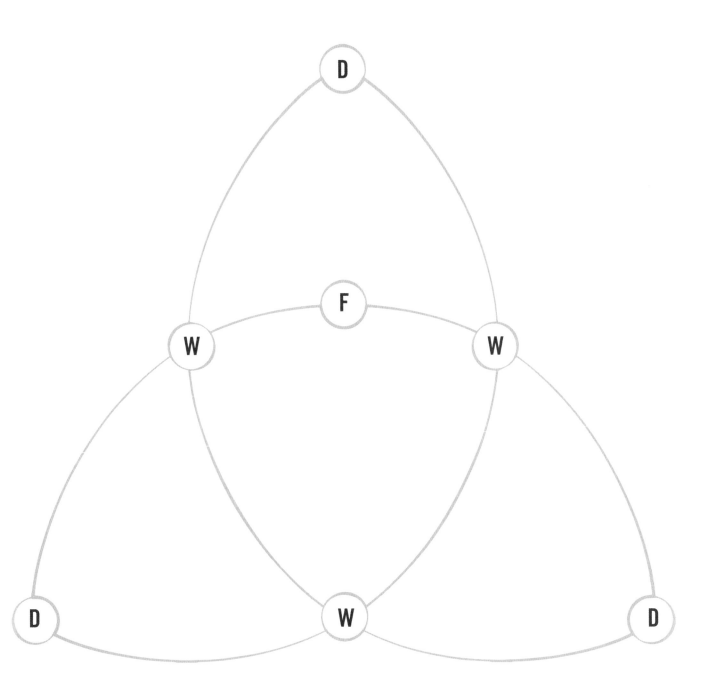

CHAPTER 3

3o HEALING CRYSTAL GRIDS TO CHANGE YOUR LIFE

In this section you
will find 30 carefully
designed crystal grids to heal
and enhance your life. Place
your crystals directly on the
page, or simply meditate on
the images with the intention
of aligning your spirit with the
energy of the grid.

GOOD LUCK GRID

PROSPERITY · FINANCIAL ABUNDANCE · GOOD FORTUNE

Built upon the highly creative Seed of Life (pages 40–41), this is an extremely powerful grid for attracting good fortune of all kinds. Use the Good Luck Grid when embarking on any new endeavor, as it has been designed to increase the odds of winning, and inspire both spiritual and material abundance. Set your intentions and expect miracles, allowing this powerful combination of crystals to focus your thoughts on manifesting divine prosperity.

Focus Stone: Amethyst (1)

True wealth flows first from the spirit, which is why your Focus Crystal is the deeply spiritual Amethyst. A highly powerful crystal for providing wisdom and spiritual insights, allow this purple gem to heighten your intuition, calm the mind, and enhance the visualization process.

Way Stone: Citrine (2)

The quickest way to good fortune is by clearing a path to joy. The golden Citrine, often referred to as the "stone of abundance," is said to be helpful in attracting and maintaining wealth, namely because of its ability to align us with the vibration of deep inner happiness. Strategically placed around the Focus Crystal on this grid (the Amethyst, which represents your spiritual center), allow the Citrine to keep you anchored in a sense of joy, leading you on the path to good fortune.

Desire Stone: Aventurine (3)

Widely known as the luckiest of all crystals, your Desire Stone is Aventurine. A very positive stone for increasing the odds of winning, allow this vibrant green gem to focus your thoughts on wealth in all its forms.

Enhancements

· Place in a quiet and clutter-free area of your home or office. A vision board or meaningful photo collage would be an excellent addition. As you pass your grid each day, focus your thoughts on each crystal and envision good fortune manifesting for you at every turn.

· This grid has been enhanced with Clear Quartz crystals that work to amplify the power of the other crystals. When pointed outward, they allow for the energy of your grid to be directed out into the Universe.

· Fresh flowers gathered from the outdoors keep the mind focused on nature's inherent capacity to renew and prosper.

· Carry the energy of this grid with you by tucking an Aventurine into your pocket during an important presentation, or by keeping it nestled in a wallet or purse to attract financial abundance.

AFFIRMATION

I choose to live in a state of constant self-renewal, and I celebrate it now.

RESTFUL SLEEP GRID

INSOMNIA · GUIDED DREAMS · DISPELLING NIGHTMARES

Built upon the Circle (pages 46–47), a powerful shape for unity and harmony, this grid is designed to promote a healthy sleep and guided dreams. Turn to this grid when you are experiencing sleep issues such as insomnia, recurrent nightmares, or trouble with falling and staying asleep.

Focus Stone: Clear Quartz Cluster (1)

One of the most powerful energy transmitters in the world, Clear Quartz is known to adapt and attune to the person using it, taking on the exact energetic frequency required for healing. When kept in the bedroom it will have a harmonizing effect on you and the environment.

Way Stone: Howlite (2)

A well-known aide for insomnia, white Howlite is widely known to improve sleep by bringing peace to the over-thinking mind. Offering a powerful link to the divine, allow it to provoke peaceful dreams that offer guidance and wisdom from your angels.

Desire Stone: Hematite (3)

Hematite is a powerful harmonizer that dissolves negative energy and prevents it from reentering the aura. Allow this black gem to dispel nightmares and guard your mind against lower thought patterns.

Enhancements

This grid has been enhanced with lavender flowers, which have long been known to help with sleep. As an addition, a few drops of lavender essential oil on the pillowcase, along with a piece of Howlite tucked within it, can work wonders to calm the mind.

AFFIRMATION

I surrender my day unto you.

3

FOCUS GRID

MENTAL CLARITY · INTELLIGENCE · ALERTNESS

Built in the shape of the simple yet very powerful Square (pages 52–53), this grid is intended to inspire mental clarity and alertness. The careful pairing of the three gems on this grid brings you the energy of peace and vibrancy. Use the Focus Grid any time you feel the need to clear yourself of mental clutter and promote quick thinking, or to take on new challenges with confidence.

Focus Stone: Blue Lace Agate (1)

A very powerful stone for the mind, Blue Lace Agate is known to inspire peace of mind and assist with self-expression. Allow this powdery blue gem to ease stress and free you from the mental burdens of old baggage, as you move forward with your daily tasks with confidence.

Way Stone: Citrine (2)

Carrying the bright and cheerful energy of the Sun, Citrine is a stone of great joy. A powerful cleanser, it is known to transmute negative energy and restore the body's chakras. It is also great for boosting creativity and helping us to connect with our intuition. Allow it to bring vibrancy to your grid.

Desire Stone: Carnelian (3)

A stone of high energy, the vibrant orange Carnelian is known to inspire intense motivation and stamina. It is also said to be helpful in inspiring a belief in one's own evaluations. Allow it to keep you clear on your desires, courageous in your pursuits, and confident in your decisions.

Enhancements

· This grid has been enhanced with Clear Quartz crystals, which will intensify and balance the energies of this grid.

· A grid associated with the mind, the Focus Grid works best when placed in an office, study, or any other room in which you spend time in deep thought. It is important to pass by this grid each morning with the intention of aligning the mind with the spirit, so grab your tea or coffee and spend a few minutes with your Focus Grid at the start of each day.

· State your affirmation at times in your day when you are feeling yourself becoming distracted or frazzled, as it will act as a powerful anchor to your inner truth.

My greatest accomplishments are made through joy and peace.

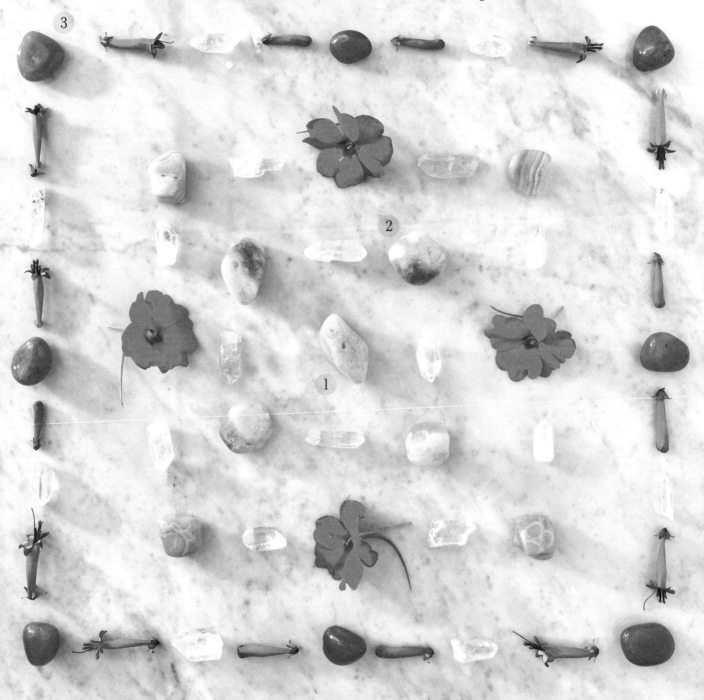

4 HEALTH GRID

ENERGY BOOST · VITALITY · MENTAL, PHYSICAL, AND SPIRITUAL WELLBEING

Built upon the ever-expanding Spiral (pages 48–49), the Health Grid is intended to remind us of our natural ability to rejuvenate. The crystals chosen for this grid are those carrying the energy of the Sun, our world's most powerful energizer. As the Sun rises each day, we are reminded that darkness is only an illusion, as only illusions can be cast away. Allow this grid to cast away all thoughts of darkness and bring forth the light, restoring you to your most healthy and harmonious state of being—mentally, physically, and spiritually. The light, after all, it is what you are made of.

Focus Stone: Amethyst (1)

A stone worn by ancient healers, some believe that placing the purple Amethyst in a window that receives sunlight can quicken the healing process. A stone of great wisdom that is good for many different uses, the Amethyst makes a natural Focus Stone for your Health Grid. Allow this deeply spiritual gem to connect you with the infinite healing power that dwells at the center of your being.

Way Stone: Citrine (2)

Joy is the quickest way to miracles, which makes Citrine a wonderful choice on a health grid. Carrying the energy of the Sun, the golden Citrine is known for its ability to lighten moods and provoke a deep sense of happiness. A powerful energizer, emotionally and physically, allow the Citrine to align your heart, body, and soul with the energy of pure joy.

Desire Stone: Ametrine (3)

The desire for any health-related goal would be to become wholly aligned. Embodying the state of complete alignment, the Ametrine is a powerful blend of Amethyst and Citrine. This gold and purple stone is said to work as a powerful cleanser, by dispersing negative energy from the aura.

Enhancements

- Build this grid in a brightly lit space, preferably close to a window, or outside in the sun.

- Enhance with anything that makes you feel joyful and connected to consciousness. The sunflower is placed here because of its happy color and ability to always invoke a smile.

72

AFFIRMATION

I choose to dwell in the restorative light of my inner being, for this is what I am.

5 POWER GRID

Built upon the shape of the Ashoka Chakra (pages 58–59), which holds the energy of the most sacred moral virtues, the Power Grid is intended to offer an extra jolt of courage, motivation, and protection. Use this grid when you are embarking on a journey that requires your highest levels of willpower and strength.

Focus Stone: Amethyst (1)

The purple Amethyst is believed to encourage deep spiritual wisdom, the true foundation for all strength and power. Acting as the Focus Stone for this grid, Amethyst offers spiritual protection and helps us to guard ourselves against overindulgences. Allow it to inspire a sense of spiritual connection and promote guided decision-making.

Way Stone: Obsidian Arrowhead (2)

A natural symbol for self-control and resilience, the Obsidian Arrowhead was used in battle thousands of years ago. This sharp, black stone is a natural Way Stone for this grid because it effectively points the way to building determination, easing fear, and guarding against all forms of negativity.

Desire Stone: Carnelian (3)

Worn around the necks of ancient warriors as an amulet for protection, the vibrant, orange Carnelian is a useful stone for building courage. When placed along the outer edges of this grid, it offers powerful energetic support for increased stamina, boldness, and motivation.

Enhancements

· This grid is best built in an area where you will often see it, such as an office or a powder room. Please note, however, that it should not be placed in the bedroom, as its vibrant energy could have a negative effect on your sleep.

· Decorate this grid with brightly colored flower petals or foliage. Bright colors such as red, yellow, and orange encourage happiness, vibrancy, strength, energy boosts, excitement, courage, and motivation.

· If you own a special piece of jewelry that you wear daily, place it on the Amethyst Focus Stone overnight to charge it with the energy of the grid, and wear it the following day.

I am bold and brave. I embrace each new circumstance with love.

6 CREATIVITY GRID

Built upon the Star of David (pages 56–57), a shape of balance, purpose, and discovery, this grid is intended to direct your focus inward to receive new ideas and insights. Turn to the Creativity Grid any time you feel stuck on a creative project, or would benefit from a boost of creativity, as the vibrant and soothing energies of these crystals will help shift your perception, allowing you to see in exciting new ways.

Focus Stone: Peacock Ore (1)

Peacock Ore encourages us to be flexible in our thinking and supports the flow of new ideas. A stone of innovation, it is known to provoke revolutionary insights that can often arise very suddenly. Allow this gem to promote fresh ways of thinking.

Way Stone: Aventurine (2)

A stone of luck and abundance, the green Aventurine enhances our creativity by helping us to be both decisive and persevering. Allow it to help move you past what is blocking you.

Desire Stone: Pyrite (3)

A stone of endless possibilities, Pyrite is known to be helpful in allowing us to take on large concepts and ideas. This golden gem is believed to infuse its surroundings with positive energy and offer a boost of confidence to its owner. As a Desire Stone, it helps us to see the big picture, and know that we are worthy and capable of achieving our goals.

Enhancements

- Kyanite has been placed around the center of the grid to inspire a sense of harmony and wellbeing. This powerful blue blade is known to instantly align the body's chakras, and is one of the few stones that has the ability to cleanse other gems. Allow it to help release any blocks and keep your energy aligned.

- This grid has been decorated with the feather of a peacock, as the unique eye of the peacock feather is known as a powerful symbol for creative vision and awakening.

76

AFFIRMATION

I am a divine creation, creating divine creations.

7

SUCCESS GRID

CAREER PROGRESS · GOAL ATTAINMENT · IGNITING PASSION

Built upon the productive Seed of Life (pages 40–41), the Success Grid is intended to spark your innermost desires with intense ferocity. The crystals chosen for this grid each represent, in one way or another, the element of fire, carrying with them the energy of passion and progress. Allow this grid to ignite within you a sense of creative passion that propels you like a wildfire toward your goals.

Focus Stone: Pyrite (1)

Naturally, the Focus Stone for this grid is a cluster of golden Pyrite. Named for its ability to spark fire when struck, allow this gem to inspire the flow of ideas and help you to carry your goals through to completion.

Way Stone: Fire Agate (2)

The iridescent, brown Fire Agate brings the energy of progression and advancement to your grid, helping you to take the steps toward success. This gem is also known to symbolize the inherent perfection of the spirit. Allow it to serve as a reminder of the divine and unstoppable flame that burns within you.

Desire Stone: Jet (3)

Formed out of fossilized wood, but looking more like a lump of coal, Jet is said to dispel negativity, stabilize finances, and offer protection, especially in the realm of business. Lining the outer edges of your grid with its protective energy, allow this black gem to inspire a sense of courage and strength in your endeavors.

Enhancements

· Ideally, this grid should be built where you most frequently work. For most of us, this will be our office, but if you work most often somewhere else (I snuggle into a chaise longue in the sun when writing and responding to emails, for example), then set up your grid there instead.

· Four additional pieces of Pyrite have been placed close to the Fire Agate stones (our stone for progression), with the intention of offering an extra boost of positivity to your daily actions. Clear Quartz crystals have been placed freely across the grid to amplify the energy of the other stones. They are pointed outward, as a symbol of the energy projecting into the Universe.

· Decorate this grid with fiery, intensely colored foliage to inspire courage, stamina, and passion.

AFFIRMATION

My dreams are ignited. I am the light of my way.

8

FRIENDSHIP GRID

CONNECTION · HARMONY · COOPERATION

Built upon the great balancing forces of the Borromean Rings (pages 60–61), this grid is designed to inspire harmonious communion. Offering the energies of love, laughter, and forgiveness, the Friendship Grid can be applied with the intention of deepening connections with existing family, friends, and coworkers, or it can be used to attract meaningful relationships to your life.

Focus Stone: Rose Quartz (1)

At the center of all great friendships is a solid foundation of love, which is why Rose Quartz is the perfect Focus Stone for your Friendship Grid. Often referred to as "the stone of unconditional love," allow this pink beauty to open your heart chakra to receiving more love.

Way Stone: Pyrite (2)

Infused with positive energy, the golden Pyrite is a powerful conduit for joy. It is known to boost self-worth, shield us from negativity, and inspire positive thoughts. Just like a great friend who can always make us laugh, Pyrite can be kept and carried to lighten your mood and alleviate unwanted thoughts.

Desire Stone: Beryl (3)

The beautiful aqua-blue Beryl is a powerful harmonizer. It opens the mind and helps us to take in a variety of different perspectives, bridging gaps and allowing for compassion and forgiveness. As a Desire Stone on a Friendship Grid, it helps us to cut through any differences and stay focused on the goal of building loving relationships.

Enhancements

· Building a crystal grid with a friend or partner can act as a powerful healing ritual. If there is a specific relationship you wish to enhance, why not ask this person to join you? If that isn't a possibility, writing this person's name on a piece of paper and placing it underneath your grid will focus your grid's energy on this particular relationship.

· When you are finished with your Friendship Grid, you might want to gift a few of these gems to a special person in your life.

I love myself, just as I love you. There is only love between us.

9 FINDING DIRECTION GRID

LIFE PURPOSE · COURSE CORRECTION · CLARITY

There are times in life when we feel lost without a direction, not knowing what to seek or even what to pray for. Built upon the sacred Flower of Life (pages 42–43), a shape carrying the energy of self-knowledge, this grid is intended to shift your focus inward, revealing your highest calling.

Focus Stone: Clear Quartz Cluster (1)

Clear Quartz is an incredibly powerful stone that is known to fine-tune its vibration for the specific needs of its owner. The sparkly cluster will zero in on your needs and what might be blocking you, and will help to lift your spirits to a higher level.

Way Stone: Beryl (2)

Beryl is the stone for refinement, helping us to shed all unnecessary baggage and focus only on that which will lead us to achieving our highest potential. Allow it to clear mental clutter and confusion and help you to see a clear path before you.

Desire Stone: Amethyst (3)

Known for its sobering effect, Amethyst has the ability to guard against overindulgences. In fact, in ancient times this purple gem was worn to prevent drunkenness. Allow it to promote deep spiritual wisdom and guided decision-making.

Enhancements

· Build this grid in a quiet place where it won't be disturbed, decorating it with anything that gives you a sense of meaning, purpose, or direction.

· A feather, a cross, or a compass are all wonderful items that you might choose to represent purpose and direction. Visit this grid once in the morning and once before bed, making sure to repeat the affirmation each time.

AFFIRMATION

In faith, I know that the steps I take are guided.

82

10 "GOOD FOR ANYTHING" GRID

ALL PURPOSES · PROGRAM WITH ANY DESIRE OR INTENTION

In a hurry? Don't have the right crystals on hand? Not to worry—there is a crystal grid to cover these scenarios! I love this grid because not only can it be used for a variety of different purposes, it is also very practical—you don't have to own a huge and expensive crystal collection in order to build it. Simply get your hands on a small bag of Amethyst and Clear Quartz and you're all set to build any type of crystal grid. This grid in particular uses the Flower of Life shape (pages 40–41) with a few small variations on stone placement. Feel free to get creative and place your gems anywhere that feels right. Remember, this is *your* grid!

Focus Stone: Clear Quartz (1)

Clear Quartz is an amazing all-purpose crystal because of its ability to take on energy. Simply hold your Clear Quartz close to your heart while thinking of the unique intention or desire you wish for it to hold. Focus Stones are for keeping us centered on what is most important, so keep this in mind while charging your Clear Quartz.

Way Stone: Amethyst (2)

In addition to having a wide variety of different meanings and uses, Amethyst is a highly spiritual stone that will adapt to your needs by providing spiritual insights for any given situation. Allow it to shift your focus inward and offer deep spiritual wisdom.

Desire Stone: Clear Quartz (3)

Repeated on this grid because of its ability to adapt to our needs, program your Clear Quartz Desire Stones with your innermost desire for this situation.

Enhancements

A Clear Quartz cluster has been used as the Focus Stone for this grid, but any tumbled or raw Clear Quartz will do. If you are using Clear Quartz points as your Way or Desire Stones, face them outward, to send the energy out into the Universe. Doing so is especially helpful if you are aiming to achieve a specific outcome or goal. If it is an internal change you are seeking, face your points inward, and they will help to direct the grid's energy toward you.

84

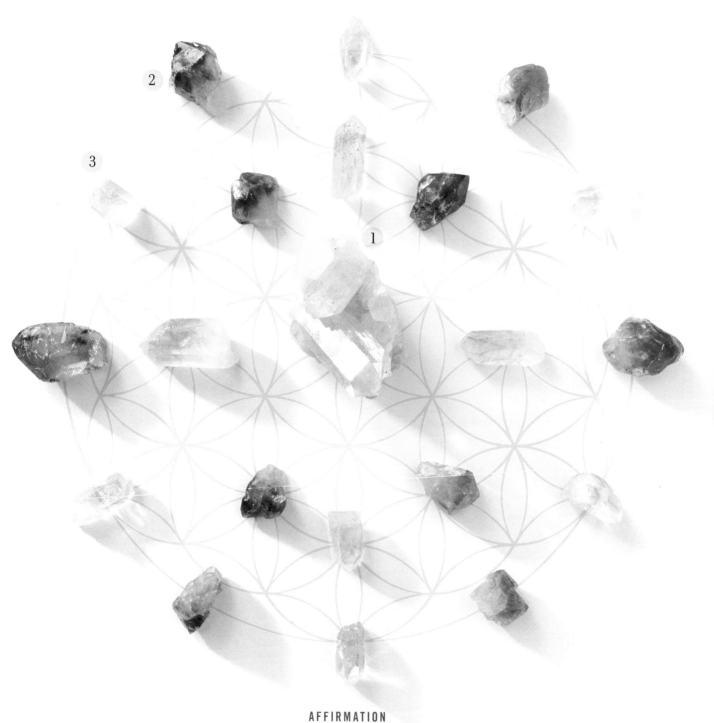

11

BREAKTHROUGH GRID

ACHIEVING SUCCESS · BREAKING OUT OF FEAR · OVERCOMING OBSTACLES

Built upon the Tripod of Life (pages 62–63), a shape associated with creation, rebirth, and transformation, the Breakthrough Grid is intended to awaken your ability to break free from what holds you back. Use the grid when you perceive yourself as trapped, stalled, or stuck; it will help you to see the most joyful way through challenges and obstacles.

Focus Stone: Angelite (1)

A stone associated with miracles, Angelite is at the center of your Breakthrough Grid. This blue gem is believed to help us to connect with intuition and communicate with our angels. Allow it to keep you focused on divine solutions.

Way Stone: Moonstone (2)

Widely known as "the stone of new beginnings," Moonstone is another stone that connects us to our intuition and provides emotional clarity. As the Way Stone for this grid, it is intended to provide necessary insights that will forge a path beyond fear and into a greater sense of joy and peace.

Desire Stone: Citrine (3)

Often referred to as "the stone of abundance," Citrine is an amazing stone for attracting good fortune of all kinds. As a Desire Stone for this grid, it points the way to miracles, and opens us to experiencing true joy.

Enhancements

· Drawing a connecting line between crystals, this grid has been enhanced with 14 small Citrine crystals and one Clear Quartz wand, representing the illumination of your new path.

· Build this grid in an intimate space, making time each day to center your thoughts on the golden pathway before you. Visualize yourself walking down this pathway, one that leads to a bright white light of peace and joy. Feel all fear wash away as you step into this light and allow it to cleanse you, knowing that freedom from fear is the truest form of breakthrough.

AFFIRMATION

My path is lit with divine solutions, and I choose to see them now.

12

GOOD VIBES GRID

JOY · POSITIVITY · GOOD FORTUNE

Built in the balancing and harmonious shape of the Circle (pages 46–47), this grid is intended to inspire positivity of all kinds. Turn to the Good Vibes Grid any time you wish to add positive energy to an area of your life, from inspiring good fortune on a new career path, through the purchasing of a new home, to enhancing your love life. The Good Vibes grid is a wonderfully flexible grid that can be applied to many different circumstances.

Focus Stone: Pyrite (1)

A stone of great positivity, the shimmering golden Pyrite is known to energize its surroundings and offer a shield of protection from negativity. As a Focus Stone, it will help to guard your thoughts and keep you in a state of heightened awareness.

Way Stone: Rose Quartz (2)

Rose Quartz adds harmony to your Good Vibes Grid. A stone of unconditional love, Rose Quartz is known to balance the emotions and inspire deep inner peace. It helps us to stay centered and open to receiving love in all forms.

Desire Stone: Aventurine (3)

Widely known as the luckiest of all gems, Aventurine will attract good favor of all kinds. This vivid green gem is known to enhance financial prosperity, offer support for important presentations and performances, and inspire us to heal physically. As a Desire Stone on your Good Vibes Grid, it promotes a general feeling of wellbeing.

Enhancement (4)

This grid has been enhanced with 14 small pieces of Citrine. A stone of great joy, Citrine is a powerful energizer and rejuvenator that is said to carry the energy of the Sun. As an addition to this grid, it is a symbol of your path being lined with gold. Take joy in knowing that you are guided along every step of your journey.

AFFIRMATION

Every day, in every way, I am delighted with good favor.

13

ROMANCE GRID

ATTRACT LOVE · INCREASE PASSION · IMPROVE A ROMANTIC CONNECTION

Built upon the harmonizing Vesica Piscis (pages 44–45), this grid is intended to inspire deep and meaningful romantic connections. Use the Romance Grid to increase passion with an existing partner, or for help in attracting new love.

Focus Stone: Clear Quartz Heart (1)

Every relationship is perfectly unique, which is why the Clear Quartz Heart makes an ideal Focus Stone for this grid. Clear Quartz can be charged with any desire or intention. Simply hold your Clear Quartz Heart before setting your grid and think of the type of relationship you wish to manifest.

Way Stone: Garnet (2)

Like a great partner, Garnet has the ability to read our emotions and provoke passion or serenity as needed. Allow it to help guide your emotions and make any necessary energetic shifts.

Desire Stone: Rose Quartz (3)

Of course, there is no better Desire Stone for a Romance Grid than the stone of unconditional love. Allow the soft pink Rose Quartz to soothe the emotions and open the heart to receiving love.

Enhancements

· Often associated with Venus, the goddess of love, the pinecone is a symbol for sexuality. Containing the shape of the ever-expanding Spiral, the pinecone has been added to increase passion.

· This grid is best built in a bedroom. If you are in a relationship, building this grid with your partner can act as a powerful bonding activity, especially if you both commit to repeating the affirmation daily. Post it on a mirror or save it to your phone as a reminder.

AFFIRMATION

I am grateful for the love that finds me, now and forever. Amen.

14

WISDOM GRID

KNOWLEDGE · CLARITY · INTUITION

Built on the simple, serene, and balancing Triangle (pages 50–51), this grid is intended to pull the energies of the mind, body, and spirit into alignment, to provide us with deep spiritual insights. Use this grid when you are in need of answers; it has been created to help us in knowing the complete truth of a situation.

Focus Stone: Apophyllite (1)

The sparkling Apophyllite is believed to instantly uplift the energy of its surroundings. When used in meditation, it is believed to help us to connect to divine inspiration and is often used by psychics to see into the future. Allow it to provide immediate clarity.

Way Stone: Moonstone (2)

Leading the way to deeper insights is the highly intuitive Moonstone. Known for its connection to the Moon, this creamy, caramel-colored gem is believed to soothe the emotions and put us in touch with our subconscious thought patterns.

Desire Stone: Howlite (3)

White Howlite is known to calm the mind and open us up to receiving spiritual insights. If you are facing any kind of confusion, worry, or anger, it is believed to absorb these negative thoughts and replace them with a sense of serenity.

Enhancement

This grid has been enhanced with a feather, a powerful symbol of wisdom. Since birds fly high up in the sky, the feather has long been used as a representational gateway to the spirit world, aiding communication to a higher plane. Feathers can also symbolize a spiritual journey.

AFFIRMATION

I tune in to higher wisdom now. Let there be light.

15

PURIFICATION GRID

STRESS RELEASE · REJUVENATION · ENERGETIC DETOXIFICATION

Carrying the cleansing and soothing energy of the ocean, the Purification Grid is intended to restore, renew, and rejuvenate. Built upon the shape of the Spiral (pages 48–49), which expands out into the infinite, turn to this grid when you feel off-kilter energetically. Focus on this grid to release and restore your energetic body.

Focus Stone: Citrine (1)

Carrying the energy of the Sun, Citrine is a powerful cleanser and rejuvenator. It helps to both enhance joy and cleanse us of unwanted energy. As a Focus Stone, it awakens you to your natural state, which is divine and perfect health in all ways.

Way Stone: Blue Lace Agate (2)

Very much like the gentle sound of the waves washing up on the shore, Blue Lace Agate offers us its peaceful and soothing energy. It is known to help with releasing unwanted emotions through the expression of our feelings. Since, most often, stress and anxiety are caused by repressed feelings, Blue Lace Agate is a natural Way Stone for the Purification Grid, helping us to find new and healthy ways to release tension.

Desire Stone: Kyanite (3)

Kyanite is an amazing stone for attuning us to higher frequencies. It is known to cut through that which blocks us and restore our energy. When held, Kyanite will instantly align the body's chakras, making it a very effective stone for use in any form of healing.

Enhancements

· This grid has been enhanced with 10 smaller Citrine crystals to symbolize the infinite joy that is of our essence. Seashells have been added to bring forth the soothing energy of the ocean.

· The Purification Grid is best built next to water, so place it in your favorite spot next to a pond or lake, or even next to your bathtub, to symbolize stress and negativity being washed away.

16 STAMINA GRID

PROGRESSION · ENERGY BOOST · DETERMINATION

Built upon the Seed of Life (pages 40–41), which helps us in the realm of creative expansion, this grid is designed to offer support as we journey toward achieving our goals. Turn to the Stamina Grid any time you find yourself saying things like "I'm too tired/stressed/exhausted," or "I can't handle this stress," as this is the perfect grid for offering the energy we need to push through to the finish line.

Focus Stone: Selenite Tower (1)

Holding a very powerful vibration for peace, Selenite is known to connect us with angelic realms. It cuts through confusion and helps us to maintain clarity. As a Focus Stone, allow it to dispel stress and keep your sights set on the task at hand.

Way Stone: Fire Agate (2)

A stone of advancement and progression, Fire Agate offers us energetic support through challenging situations. It offers us the energy to carry forward, even when we no longer feel a sense of motivation.

Desire Stone: Ametrine (3)

A powerful combination of Amethyst and Citrine, Ametrine is a natural rejuvenator. Being a combination of the two stones, it carries the energy of the complete harmony of mind, body, and spirit. As a Desire Stone, it represents the completion of important tasks.

Enhancements

· This grid has been enhanced with eight pieces of Citrine—a powerful energizer that is known to promote joy, stamina, and health. When added to the outer parts of the Seed of Life shape, Citrine pulls our focus toward these qualities and can help us to manifest joy in our end result.

· This grid is best built in a room where you most often work. Visit your grid and repeat its accompanying affirmation before and after performing important tasks.

96

AFFIRMATION

I come to life with the energy of spirit,
completing all tasks.

17 BLESSED HOME GRID

Built upon the Circle (pages 46–47), a shape of harmony, unity, and balance, the Blessed Home Grid is created with the intention of clearing our homes of unwanted energies and refreshing them with the energies for joy and peace. Use this grid to bless a new home, or to cleanse and clear your current dwelling.

Focus Stone: Selenite Mini Tower (1)

When Selenite is placed in the home, it is known to promote a peaceful atmosphere. Allow it to center your thoughts on creating a serene environment for yourself and your loved ones.

Way Stone: Selenite (2)

Selenite has also been chosen for the Way Stone on this grid because of its ability to guard and protect. While the Selenite Focus Stone keeps us centered, the smaller pieces line the outer edges, creating a protective shield around your home.

Desire Stone: Citrine (3)

A stone of great joy, the Citrine is a powerful regenerator and rejuvenator. As the Desire Stone for this grid, it warms the home and promotes a sense of joy. It is also known to attract wealth and abundance.

Enhancements

· This grid has been enhanced with feathers and twigs to symbolize the bird's nest, a powerful symbol for a safe, secure resting place. Simply replicate a nest by tying vine stems and twigs together with natural twine. Just as a bird builds her nest from materials she has gathered herself, decorate this grid with meaningful objects that represent comfort and love for you.

· Adding flowers in small vases is an effective way of helping them to last longer (although it does not matter if the flowers dry out in the duration of the grid).

· Build this grid in the furthest left corner of your home (in relation to the front door), and the Citrine will become a powerful attractor for wealth and abundance, according to the principles of Feng Shui.

18 NEW BEGINNINGS GRID

COURAGE · STABILITY · PROTECTION

Combining the energies of the Cross and the Circle (pages 54–55 and 46–47), this grid is designed to offer a sense of courage, protection, and harmony in all new endeavors. Turn to this grid when embarking on a new path, such as a new career, a new relationship, or any other life change, big or small. The New Beginnings Grid will offer support in releasing the past, while promoting a swift and safe transition into new territories.

Focus Stone: Citrine Cluster (1)

A powerful transmitter of joy, Citrine is known to both energize and cleanse the energetic body. Allow it to boost energy levels and inspire a deep sense of spiritual, emotional, and mental wellbeing as you embark on your new journey.

Way Stone: Aquamarine (2)

In ancient times, the blue-green Aquamarine was carried by sailors for good luck and protection. As a Way Stone for your grid, it guides you with the energy of courage, clarity, and faith.

Desire Stone: Moonstone (3)

Often referred to as "the stone of new beginnings," Moonstone is known to calm the emotions and help us to connect to our intuition. Allow it to provide guidance and ease the stress that can so often come with new transitions.

Enhancements

· This grid has been enhanced with nine additional pieces of Moonstone that form the shape of a semicircle around the bottom half of the grid. They were placed with the intention of creating an anchor-like shape to represent the fact that we are always safely anchored in spirit. Clear Quartz has also been added around the center, to amplify the effects of the grid.

· As always, be creative in how you place your stones. Remember, this is your unique creation, and the only rule you must follow is that it means something to you.

AFFIRMATION

I am free to go with the flow, as I am always safely anchored in spirit.

19

PROTECTION GRID

SECURITY · STABILITY · DISPEL NEGATIVE ENERGY

Forming a powerful shield in the shape of the Square (pages 52–53), the Protection Grid is intended to inspire a deep sense of safety and security. Choose this grid any time you feel unsafe, whether physically or energetically. The crystals on this grid have been selected to shield you from many different types of misfortune.

Focus Stone: Jet (1)

Formed out of fossilized wood, but looking more like a piece of coal, Jet is a highly protective stone that blocks negative energy. It is known to alleviate our fears and offer a sense of stability.

Way Stone: Jet and Rose Quartz (2)

While Jet helps to alleviate fears, Rose Quartz replaces fear with love. Known as "the stone of unconditional love," allow this soft pink gem to bring a softer energy to your grid, and to work with Jet to ease tension.

Desire Stone: Obsidian Arrowhead (3)

Formed out of molten lava that cooled too quickly to crystallize, the black Obsidian Arrowhead is fast and effective in identifying problems and going to work to remove them. When placed around the edges of your Protection Grid, it forms a powerful barrier for unwanted energies.

Enhancements

· Build this grid in a quiet part of the home where it won't be seen or disturbed (a basement works well).

· Eucalyptus has been added to this grid, as it is believed to cleanse the home of lower energies.

· If this is a protective grid for the home, an Obsidian Arrowhead can be placed under the front doormat to keep out unwanted energy.

AFFIRMATION

I surround myself with God's white light of divine love and protection. Only positive energy affects me.

20

SELF-LOVE GRID

SELF-WORTH · CONFIDENCE · PERSONAL EMPOWERMENT

Built upon the Flower of Life (pages 42–43), a shape carrying the energy for self-knowledge and introspection, this grid is intended to inspire a deep sense of inner peace and self-love. Allow the Self-Love Grid to inspire enhanced self-worth and boost confidence any time you need it.

Focus Stone: Rose Quartz (1)

Often referred to as "the stone of unconditional love," Rose Quartz is a natural Focus Stone for the Self-Love Grid. It is believed to soothe the emotions and assist in opening the heart chakra to receiving love. Allow this soft pink beauty to inspire a deep sense of self-love and inner peace.

Way Stone: Citrine (2)

An extremely invigorating stone, the golden Citrine is known for its ability to elevate moods, bolster willpower, and enhance mental clarity. A powerful energizer, emotionally and physically, allow the Citrine to empower you with a deep sense of confidence.

Desire Stone: Amethyst (3)

One of the most powerful crystals on the planet, the purple Amethyst is known to promote wisdom, spiritual growth, and enlightenment. As a Desire Stone it strengthens your crown chakra and thus your connection to the divine, which is truly the greatest kind of empowerment there is.

Enhancements

· Place this grid in an intimate part of the home, such as in a bedroom or powder room where you will often see it.

· This grid has been enhanced with flowers, leaves, rose petals, and Clear Quartz. The rosebud is a symbol for purity and love, reminding us that the value of a rose does not change from bud to bloom. Your value is inherent, and you are worthy in all of your glorious stages of beauty.

· Your Focus Stone, the Rose Quartz, is known to enhance the power of positive affirmations, so repeat your self-love affirmation several times throughout the day, especially before bed and first thing each morning, to allow the message of self-love to take root deep in the subconscious mind.

AFFIRMATION

I am whole and complete, from bud to bloom.
I approve of myself, and I am enough.

21

STRESS RELEASE GRID

RELEASING ANXIETY · ALLEVIATING WORRY · ENHANCING SERENITY

Built upon the Star of David (pages 56–57), a shape that inspires us to release mental clutter and chaos, this grid is designed to help us to cut through the noise and embrace an inner state of peace. Turn to this grid any time you find yourself feeling overwhelmed, as it is intended to guide you toward simplicity, harmony, and serenity.

Focus Stone: Apophyllite (1)

Often when we are stressed, there is the desire for a quick fix—something that can guide us toward a sense of relief, and fast! Apophyllite provides great inspiration, as it is known to carry a high vibration that can immediately uplift its owner. Focus on this sparkly gem to inspire relief from worry and fear.

Way Stone: Citrine (2)

Carrying the energy of the Sun, Citrine is known to elevate moods and inspire feelings of happiness. Let this golden gem keep you rooted in a sense of inner joy, as this is the quickest way to attaining true peace.

Desire Stone: Sodalite (3)

This royal blue crystal is a powerful harmonizer, especially when it comes to helping us to release feelings of fear and anxiety. Sodalite is known to align us with our highest thoughts, and cut through mental and emotional confusion. If you suffer from panic attacks, this gem can act as a powerful helper when tucked into your purse or pocket.

Enhancement

When paired together, Citrine and Sodalite make a powerful team for combating stress. While Sodalite is known to fend off panic attacks and phobias, Citrine is a powerful rejuvenator that realigns us with our inner sense of joy. Toss these two gems into a bath with you and they will go to work to alleviate tension, worry, and fear.

AFFIRMATION

I am joy and I am peace.
My only truth is serenity.

106

22

PSYCHIC ABILITIES GRID

INTUITION · ANGELIC COMMUNICATION

Built in the shape of the unifying Circle (pages 46–47), this grid is intended to enhance intuition and psychic insights. Use this grid to increase your own psychic abilities, as we each have great power in accessing universal knowledge.

Focus Stone: Selenite Sphere (1)

Carrying a high vibration, Selenite is one of the most powerful crystals on the planet. Used for scrying by fortune-tellers and clairvoyants for thousands of years, it is known to elevate our thoughts and help us to receive divine insights.

Way Stone: Raw Selenite (2)

Seven pieces of Selenite have been added as the Way Stone for this grid. Often used on protective grids for homes, when placed around the edges of your Psychic Abilities Grid they form an energetic shield from lower entities as you open up yourself to receiving spiritual insights.

Desire Stone: Clear Quartz (3)

An energetic amplifier and harmonizer, Clear Quartz acts as the Desire Stone for this grid, enhancing the energy of the Selenite and helping to raise your vibration to the highest possible level. When pointed in the same direction going around this circle, the Clear Quartz points create a powerful energetic conductor for psychic knowledge.

Enhancements

· This grid has been decorated with pinecones, which have long been known to represent the Third Eye and our physic abilities. White flowers have been added as a symbol for purity, symbolizing the divine white light of protection that surrounds you.

· Build this grid in a quiet area of the home where it won't be disturbed by anyone, as these crystals will quickly pick up the energies of those nearby.

· Take a moment each day to sit with the crystals, quietly asking the Universe for help in receiving divine insights. Before you begin, imagine yourself surrounded with a bright white light, which will keep you safe from low-vibration entities. Gaze into your crystal ball and relax. Simply sit in peace and allow yourself to receive. You might find it helpful to use a pen and paper to free-write your thoughts. Don't try to make sense of anything—just allow whatever comes. When you are finished, thank your angels and ask that they close the circle, protecting you as you continue with the rest of your day.

AFFIRMATION

Thank you for the divine knowledge. I hear, I see, I know, I am.

STABILITY GRID

BALANCE · PROTECTION · HARMONY

There are times in life when we feel like we are on unstable ground or simply disconnected from the present moment. Built upon the naturally stabilizing Square (pages 52–53), the Stability Grid is intended to provide a sense of grounding, protection, and balance. Turn to this grid any time you feel a lack of stability, whether it is emotionally, financially, or in a relationship.

Focus Stone: Jet (1)

An incredibly grounding and stabilizing stone, Jet anchors us in the present moment and provides a sense of security. This black stone draws out negative thoughts and alleviates fears.

Way Stone: Smokey Quartz (2)

Smokey Quartz is one of the most effective stones for inspiring a sense of grounding. This gem is known to eliminate fear and anxiety, while working to realign our energetic bodies. Allow it to strengthen your connection to the physical world and help you to release negative thought patterns.

Desire Stone: Red Jasper (3)

The ultimate harmonizer, Red Jasper is believed to align the body's chakras and have a nurturing effect on its owner. Allow it to keep you rooted in a sense of balance and wellbeing.

Enhancement (4)

This grid has been enhanced with four additional pieces of tumbled Jet, to provide an added feeling of protection. Typically, when we are concerned with our stability we are battling deep-rooted fears that stem from childhood. The powerful effects of Jet on this grid will help to draw out these old thought programs and prevent further negative thinking.

AFFIRMATION

My feet are planted firmly. My heart is at ease.

24

SELF-EXPRESSION GRID

CLEAR COMMUNICATION · LIVING AUTHENTICALLY · SPEAKING ONE'S TRUTH

Built upon the Flower of Life (pages 42–43), a shape known to promote self-love and expansion, this grid is intended to help free your voice and to communicate who you are with ease. Turn to this grid for help to dispel fears relating to communication, or to live authentically, as the crystals have been carefully chosen to help align mind, body, and spirit with the energy of love.

Focus Stone: Clear Quartz Heart (1)

The Clear Quartz Heart is placed as the Focus Stone for this grid, to remind you to give your heart what it truly needs: your unconditional approval. Known to take on the energy of our thoughts and intentions, program your Clear Quartz Heart with your most loving intentions for yourself.

Way Stone: Blue Lace Agate (2)

One of the very best stones for clear communication, this powdery blue gem is known to clear the throat chakra, the center for communication, and help us to release the fear of judgment, so that we can express ourselves fully.

Desire Stone: Rose Quartz (3)

A stone of unconditional love and peace, Rose Quartz leads us on a path of self-love. Allow this pink gem to inspire complete emotional balance and harmony.

Enhancement (4)

This grid has been enhanced with four Kyanite blades. Known to cut through emotional blocks and align the body's chakras, allow the grid to help you release anything and everything that has kept you from expressing yourself fully.

AFFIRMATION

I speak freely with the voice of love. I express myself with ease, poise, and grace.

25

MOTHERHOOD GRID

Built upon the unifying Borromean Rings (pages 60–61), this grid is designed to inspire health, strength, and wellness as they relate to motherhood. Both new and experienced moms may turn to this grid for help with solving parenting issues, balancing female hormones, promoting self-care, and releasing the various types of stress related to parenting. This is also a wonderful grid to build when pregnant or trying to conceive.

Focus Stone: Clear Quartz Heart (1)

Before you can most effectively care for another human being, you must be sure to take care of yourself. The Clear Quartz Heart is placed as the Focus Stone for this grid to help remind you that your needs are important. Just like any great mom, the Clear Quartz is known to attune its energy to the needs of its recipient. Release all guilt in fulfilling your own needs, and program this gem with love and positive intentions for yourself.

Way Stone: Moonstone (2)

Often called "the stone of motherhood," the creamy, caramel-colored Moonstone is believed to be a powerful healing gem for women—balancing hormones, relieving stress, and invoking deep spiritual insights. Allow it to inspire complete spiritual and emotional harmony.

Desire Stone: Desert Rose (3)

With a flower-like shape that has been etched slowly over time by millions of grains of desert sand, the Desert Rose is a true masterpiece of Mother Nature. This artful gem is believed to quiet worries and promote mental clarity. Allow it to help you cut through all tension and stress.

Enhancements

· This grid has been enhanced with additional pieces of Moonstone, Clear Quartz, and Rose Quartz along the edges of the rings to create a unified path of energy. You may also want to add other items of significance, such as a small drawing made by your child, a photo, or even a locket of your child's hair.

· Acorns have been used here as a symbol of motherhood and growth: "Mighty oaks from little acorns grow," so says the proverb.

AFFIRMATION

I am love. I am blessed. I am a blessing.

26

FORGIVENESS GRID

OVERCOMING HEARTACHE · LETTING GO · CORD-CUTTING

Built on the extremely powerful Cross (pages 54–55), a shape holding the energy for atonement, this grid is intended to help us to release grievances. Turn to the Forgiveness Grid for help with letting go of the mistakes of others, or for when you need help to forgive yourself. It is also helpful for letting go of childhood traumas.

Focus Stone: Amethyst Cluster (1)

A highly spiritual stone, Amethyst is known for its protective abilities—spiritually, emotionally, and mentally. It is said to balance the emotions, dispel negativity, and guard against overindulgences. It helps us to stay centered on the spiritual truth of the situation, allowing us to release negative thought patterns.

Way Stone: Rose Quartz (2)

Acting as the Way Stone for your Forgiveness Grid, the Rose Quartz helps to open the door to love. It helps us to release old wounds, balance our emotions, and love without condition.

Desire Stone: Obsidian Arrowhead (3)

Pointed outward as the Desire Stone for your Forgiveness Grid, the Obsidian Arrowhead represents the removal of all barriers. A stone of great truth, it is known to slice through obstacles instantaneously. Allow it to inspire the release of fear and illusion.

Enhancements

· This grid has been enhanced with four additional Amethyst points around the center. They are outward facing to represent the disbursement and release of pain.

· Build your Forgiveness Grid in a private space, being sure to pass by it daily. Repeat the accompanying affirmation as many times as you can throughout the day. You will know you are finished with this grid when you feel a sense of peace for the situation.

AFFIRMATION

I am a house for love. Nothing else can live here. I release you (this situation) with love and I let you (it) go in peace.

27 OVERCOMING ADDICTIONS GRID

BREAKING HABITS · LIFESTYLE IMPROVEMENTS · RELEASING TOXICITY

Built upon the Star of David (pages 56-57), a shape for easing stress and connecting with our inner spirit, this grid is intended to help with the releasing of toxic patterns, habits, and addictions. In our hectic and stressful daily lives, it is common to seek escape in things like food, phones, substances, and even people. Whether an unproductive habit is mild or serious, we always have the power to change it. Allow this grid to help you to take charge of your patterns, and make new and more empowering decisions.

Focus Stone: Amethyst Cluster (1)

A stone frequently used for help in overcoming addictions, Amethyst is known to have a sobering effect on its owner. It distills our thought processes and helps us to make responsible decisions. Allow this purple gem to inspire wise choices and replace pain patterns with a deeper sense of spiritual connection.

Way Stone: Rose Quartz (2)

At the root of any poor choice or addiction is the suppression and avoidance of pain. Known as "the stone of unconditional love," allow the Rose Quartz to open your heart chakra, so that you can feel and release your pain.

Desire Stone: Amethyst Points (3)

Amethyst is such a powerful stone for overcoming addictions that it is used twice on this grid. It goes to work on old wounds and helps us to release them. This purple stone is highly restorative and will work to heal on emotional, spiritual, and physical levels.

Enhancements

· This grid has been enhanced with 11 smaller Amethyst points. Eleven is the number of spiritual awakening and, when repeated with the placement of the Amethyst, it creates a powerful conductor of healing energy that assists us in transmuting pain into peace.

· Any time you feel the urge to repeat an unhealthy habit, sit quietly with your grid and envision yourself sitting on a bridge that overlooks a river. As you allow yourself to experience your discomfort, watch the river run murky and unclear. Feel any pain that enters and, when you are ready to let go, see in your mind's eye the river gradually turning from muddy to clear and pristine. Repeat your affirmation several times throughout the day.

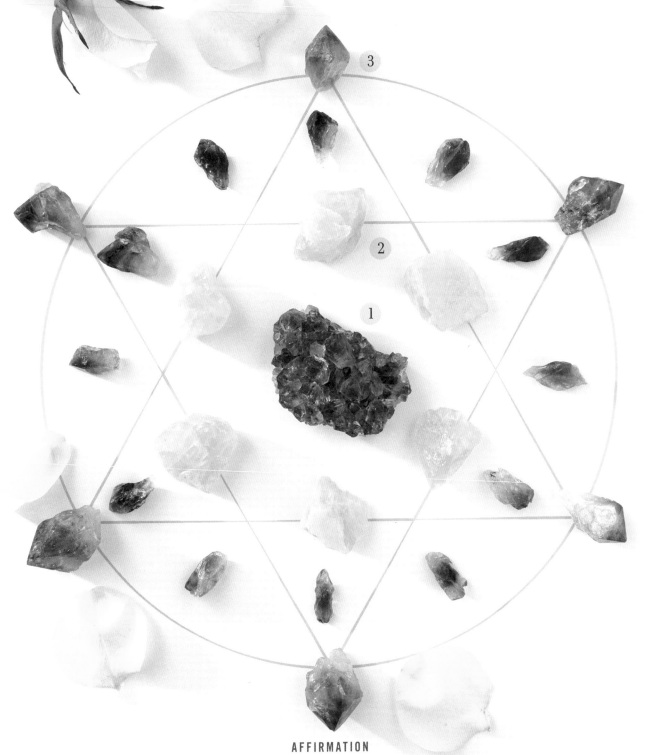

AFFIRMATION

I let go and allow these feelings of pain to move through me now.
I am the bridge, not the river.

28

BROKEN HEART GRID

CORD-CUTTING · RELEASING THE PAST · EMOTIONAL HEALING

Built upon the Vesica Piscis (pages 44–45), a shape of rebirth and transformation, the Broken Heart Grid is intended to restore harmony and balance to the aching heart. Turn to this grid to release an ex-partner, rebuild self-worth, heal old wounds, or to repair a relationship that has been damaged.

Focus Stone: Clear Quartz Heart (1)

Representing the unique beauty of your own heart, the powerful Clear Quartz Heart is known to attune to the specific needs of its owner. Program this gem with any desire or intention, and allow it to assist in transmuting all lower energy into love and light.

Way Stone: Beryl (2)

The teal-colored Beryl is a powerful stone for helping us to shed all unnecessary baggage. It will assist in the release of old patterns and wounds, while helping to forge a new path for yourself.

Desire Stone: Rose Quartz (3)

Naturally, the Desire Stone for this grid is the Rose Quartz, "the stone of unconditional love." This soft pink gem is known to heal the emotions and open the heart chakra to receiving new love.

Enhancements

· Tracing the edges of the Vesica Piscis are 12 small pieces of Citrine. A stone of great joy and rejuvenation, allow these gems to spark a new sense of hope and happiness within you.

· Fresh green leaves have also been added as a symbol for the renewal that is happening within your heart.

AFFIRMATION

Pain is my teacher.
I learn, love, and release.

120

29

MIRACLES GRID

ENERGY BOOST · VITALITY · MENTAL, PHYSICAL, AND SPIRITUAL WELLBEING

Built upon the Tripod of Life (pages 62–63), a shape known to carry forth its creative energies with great intensity, this grid has been designed to invoke miracles. Turn to the Miracles Grid when you have been praying for an answer but feel that you are not being heard. Rest assured that this is not the case, and, with this grid, turn your energy inward and ask that your heart be aligned with the will of the divine. This, after all, is the truest form of miracle.

Focus Stone: Angelite Cluster (1)

Known for its connection to the angelic realms, the powdery blue Angelite can be used to help inspire divine communication. Allow it to open your spirit to receiving answers and trusting that great help is on its way.

Way Stone: Angelite (2)

Because of its powerful connection to the divine, Angelite is also used as the Way Stone. This blue gem is known to calm the mind and transmute pain quickly and efficiently. Turn all worries and fears over to the angels and allow them to carry it away into the light.

Desire Stone: Shungite (3)

Often called "the stone of miracles," the carbon-based Shungite is one of the most powerful crystals in the world for healing the physical body. It is known to remove negative energy by cleansing the body's chakras. As a Desire Stone, it represents the state of divine and perfect health for mind, body, and spirit.

Enhancements

· Clear Quartz has been added freely around the center of the grid to amplify and harmonize the energy of the crystals.

· Baby's Breath has been added as an enhancement at the bottom of the grid to remind us of the miracle of life—the miracle that is you!

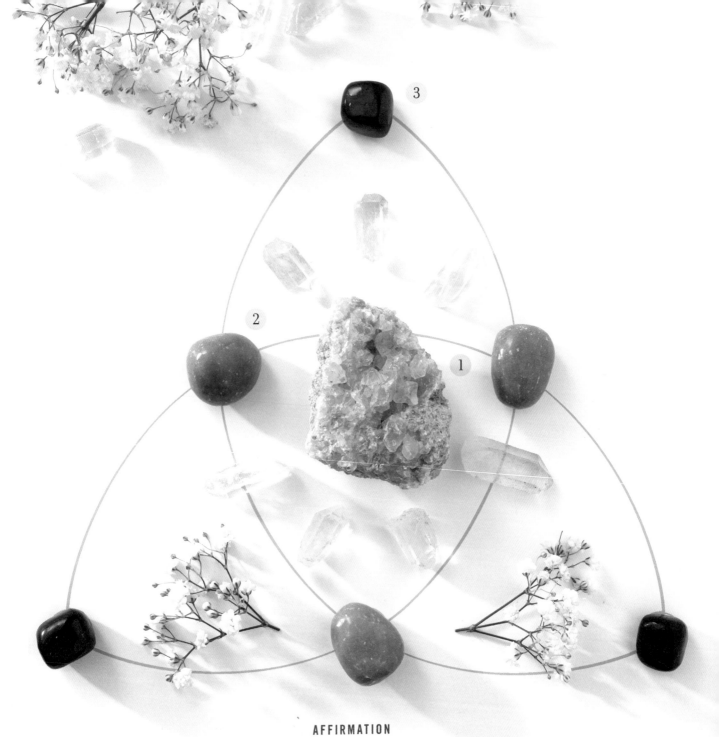

AFFIRMATION

Thank you for the miracles, all in your perfect ways,
and all in your perfect timing.

ANGELS GRID

DIVINE COMMUNICATION · ANGELIC SUPPORT · PROTECTION

Combining the energies of two very powerful shapes, the Triangle and the Circle (pages 50–51 and 46–47), this grid is intended to help call forth angelic guidance. Turn to this grid when you are in need of strength, support, or protection from the angels.

Focus Stone: Angelite Cluster (1)

Known for its connection to the angelic realms, the powdery blue Angelite offers help in receiving messages from the divine. As a Focus Stone, allow it to strengthen your faith and help you to feel the presence of angels.

Way Stone: Blue Lace Agate (2)

The throat chakra is the center for expression. When it is clear, we are not only able to hear the voice of angels, but we are also able to clearly identify our own needs. A stone of communication and self-expression, allow the Blue Lace Agate to open your centers for expression, helping you to ask the angels for what you truly need.

Desire Stone: Howlite (3)

A stone of peace and harmony, Howlite is an amazing stone for opening the mind to receiving spiritual insights. Allow this white gem to represent your prayers being heard and answered.

Enhancement

Forming a halo effect around the top of your Focus Stone, this grid has been enhanced with seven Citrine crystals. Seven is a number of high spiritual vibration and Citrine is a stone that is known to invoke great joy. Allow the powerful halo of golden gems to represent the angelic love and protection that surrounds you.

AFFIRMATION

*Thank you for surrounding me with your love and light.
I embrace your assistance with gratitude.*

INDEX

Illustrations are in *italics*.

CREDITS AND RESOURCES

The author would like to thank:
· Brooklyn Storozuk, for the author photograph on page 7
· Sydney St. Mars, for the hand photograph on page 17

Box photographs on page 12 courtesy of Little Box of Rocks
Photography pages 31,105, Emma Robinson
All other photography: Philip Wilkins
Illustrations: Kuo Kang Chen

Bibliography

The Power of Habit, Charles Duhigg (Turtleback Books, 2014)
The Crystal Bible, Judy Hall (Godsfield Press, 2003)
Crystal Grids Power, Ethan Lazzerini (CreateSpace Independent Publishing Platform, 2017)
Crystal Grids: How to Combine and Focus Crystal Energies to Enhance Your Life,
    Henry M. Mason & Brittani Petrofsky (Llewellyn Publications, U.S., 2016)
Sacred Crystals, Hazel Raven (New Burlington Press, 2017)
Sacred Geometry: Deciphering the Code, Stephen Skinner (Wooden Books, 2002)

Websites

Ancient Symbols
www.ancient-symbols.com
Looks primarily at the world's most ancient symbols, but includes a section on sacred geometry.

Crystal Vaults
www.crystalvaults.com
Shop for crystals by color, shape, or type, and enjoy some free online crystal guides.

Mesa Creative Arts
mesacreativearts.com
The website for the Spiritual Center located in Pittsburgh, Pennsylvania, includes information on classes and events, an online shop, and relevant blogs and articles.

Minerals.net
Minerals.net
Mineral and Gemstone guide, community, gallery, and research.